SS and Gestapo: rule by terror

SS and Gestapo: rule by terror

Roger Manvell Advised by Heinrich Fraenkel

Editor-in-Chief: Barrie Pitt
Art Director: Peter Dunbar
Military Consultant: Sir Basil Liddell Hart
Picture Editor: Bobby Hunt
Executive Editor: David Mason
Designer: Sarah Kingham
Research Assistant: Yvonne Marsh
Cartographer: Richard Natkiel
Special Drawings: John Batchelor

ISBN 0-345-24990-9-250

Manufactured in the United States of America

First Edition: December, 1969
Fourth Printing: April, 1976

Contents

The police state

What does it mean to live in a police state? More particularly, what did it mean to live in a police state administered by the agents and collaborators of the Nazi regime in Germany?

For those who may even now be living in something approaching such conditions, the active symptoms are only too familiar. Whoever occupies the seat of government determines the current policy for the nation, with little or no reference to the wishes of the majority of those governed. The senior officers of the bureaucracy appointed to administer the national policy – and to see that it is fulfilled through arbitrary observance of the succession of laws and decrees issued from 'on high', but not always made known to the community – hold their office not through their deserts in the public service, but because they are regarded as reliable by the governors of the state.

Behind the ranks of the normal, civic police, a second, perhaps much larger contingent of secret, political police is added to act as the strong arm for the new law, providing the spies and watchdogs for the bureaucracy. The prisons, and certain penal establishments which may be set up (such as concentration camps for the rehabilitation of 'backsliders') begin to fill with those whose loyalty to the regime has been found wanting. There they may wait under duress and without trial, subject to constant, punitive interrogation to wrest from them what they are thought to know about others who represent resistance in the eyes of the authorities.

This is not the end of the story. In a police state, nothing in the community can be considered stable, except by virtue of brute force or the exercise of a Machiavellian ability by the powerful to keep themselves in office. In a police state everyone, whatever his status, is potentially a suspect, everyone is tabbed on a secret file which records whether he may be considered loyal or disloyal to the regime. Today's interrogator may be tomorrow's prisoner, following some sudden, unexpected 'palace revolution' or some shift in power at departmental level. Even among the leaders themselves, someone may

suddenly disappear, while another whose face is barely known to the public takes over the vacant place.

For the ordinary citizen, living in a police state means the disappearance of most, if not all of one's civil rights. There is no protection from the peremptory knocking on the door, or the terror of sudden arrest and the disappearance of any individual, often without trace, utterly lost to his relatives and friends. The ordinary citizen who suffers from the common anxieties about the safety and security of himself and his family, soon learns to pay lip-service to the regime, and keep his nose clean. He does his daily job, performs his military service, wears the prescribed badges, pays the right dues, gives the right salutes, and keeps quiet about anything dubious he may know or suspect is going on.

As the economy of his country grows straitened through war, or the preparation for it, he learns to do without the consumer goods that other people in the state, more politically privileged than himself, may still be able to enjoy. He turns on his

The victims. Inmates of Auschwitz stare at their Russian liberators in May 1945

radio receiver, tuned to receive the national service only; like the press and publishing he knows it is strictly censored and ideologically indoctrinated. He may even for a moment wonder why it is so strictly forbidden to listen to broadcasts from abroad. If in his frustration he may grumble just a little, he refers to his leaders by initials only and speaks the words beneath his breath. He has learned always to be wary of strangers, wary of his friends, wary even of the members of his family, more especially the younger generation who have been warned to watch their parents. Above all, he is careful to let slip nothing which might be held politically suspect, let alone subversive, and he shies away from acquiring any knowledge which could conceivably be judged as dangerous. He is always the very last person to know who has just been arrested, or what they may be thought to be suffering in the concentration camps. This kind of

unpleasant business is the sole concern of the authorities. Nevertheless, he becomes the constant, if unwilling recipient of rumour; when all forms of news or information are known to be controlled or doctored, the winds of curiosity are inevitably stirred by the rustle of gossip, innuendo, and whispered warnings.

The Nazi regime created an exceptional, virulent form of police state. It stemmed directly from an exceptional, virulent ruler, who, as everyone knows, came to power in Germany in January 1933, after he was created Chancellor. Little more than a dozen years before Hitler had been living the life of a back-street agitator. Nine years before he had served a term of imprisonment for conducting an abortive, armed uprising in Munich. Once installed as Chancellor, he so rapidly entrenched himself that within months he was ruling Germany virtually by personal decree.

During his reign of terror, which lasted a bare twelve years, Hitler reformed and greatly expanded the frontiers of the German Reich, 'uniting' those whom he regarded as belonging to the common German stock, rearming his new-born nation, and, within six years, leading it into war. For a while, he became master through occupation of territory which stretched from the Arctic circle to the shores of the Mediterranean, and from the outskirts of Moscow and Leningrad to the western seaboard of France and the Low Countries. By 1942 he was in 'possession' of Norway, Denmark, Holland, Belgium, France, Luxembourg, Yugoslavia, Greece, Czechoslovakia, Poland, and a considerable area of Russia and the Ukraine, an occupation achieved within four years. Yet only three years later he was to be in hiding beneath the ruins of Berlin, master of barely a few square yards. In May 1945 he committed suicide, unable to face the final disintegration of his rule. Hitler's intervention in world history cost the lives of over fifty million, men, women, and children who died

Creators of the Police State.

Himmler and Hitler inspect an SS bodyguard, 1936

9

through battle, saturation bombing, mass-slaughter, starvation, extermination, and ill-treatment in concentration camps and prisons.

Hitler's record remains without true parallel in human history. He did what he did through the rapid establishment of a highly organized and ruthless police state. Behind the evident strength of the German army and that of the civic police stood the far less evident, and largely 'secret' forces of the SS and their colleagues of the Gestapo, the political police. Though elements in the German army serving Hitler's regime were guilty of criminal acts going far beyond the 'accepted' horrors of 'legal' total war, the crimes against humanity for which Hitler's name must stand forever execrated were undertaken in his name by these extraordinary secret forces.

It is the particular story of these secret forces which this book sets out to tell. From the smallest beginnings – a mere handful of men intended to exercise strong-arm methods to protect the speakers at Nazi rallies – the SS came to assume immeasurable power under the tutelary leadership of Heinrich Himmler, an obsessive nationalist whose gradual ascent in the Nazi hierarchy was won by backstairs intrigue. While others, notably Göring and Goebbels, expended their undoubted talents in the limelight, Himmler grew in authority with the SS forces which sustained him until he became by far the most formidable of the sub-leaders working in close association with the Führer. Unlike most of the others, Himmler had no trace of cynicism in him. He knew precisely what he believed in – the racial superiority of the Nordic, 'Aryan' peoples and the establishment of an imperial world system under German domination, the rule of the master-race.

So it was to Himmler and to certain reliable members of the SS that Hitler finally entrusted the highly secret operation of the 'final solution', the mass-extermination of the European Jews, the ultimate crime of genocide which came to a head during the middle and final years of the war. It was the SS, and in particular Himmler's deputy, Reinhard Hey-drich, who master-minded the plan for genocide which led to the mass-destruction within three years of over five million Jews and as many again of the other 'unwanted' peoples of Europe – Slavs, Gypsies, and those who for one reason or another had the fires of resistance burning in their bellies.

The SS therefore came to occupy a very special place in the Nazi conspiracy for power. In the public eye, before the war, they shone with a certain, elite splendour in their immaculate black uniforms edged with silver facings. They demonstrated, or were said to demonstrate, the glory of racial 'purity', with two full centuries of unsullied German stock standing to their credit. Lawyers and intellectuals, even certain aristocrats, let alone bishops, pulled what strings they could be admitted to the SS ranks, proud of their honorary officer status and the uniform which confirmed it. They accepted with good grace, or with a cynical humour, the bogus 'Aryan' ritual and folkloric ceremonial which Himmler had devised – as if it were the Knights of the Round Table he was convening, and not an organisation whose prime function was, in the end, to murder their fellow-men.

Certain details in this grim, extraordinary history possess a kind of dark comedy – for example, Himmler zealously competing for an SS athletics badge with his aides surreptitiously upgrading his lamentable performance, the endless fuss of racial 'purity' when any SS man felt the urge to marry, or the pagan ceremonials invented to celebrate Nazi anniversaries or replace Christian ceremonies for marriage, birth, and death. The more cynical merely laughed at Himmler behind his back, until the day came when they had to hear one of his grim speeches delivered before private gatherings of his SS officers. Here, as nowhere else, Himmler frankly outlined the need to exterminate the Jews and work his prisoners to death to further German victory. Most of them would listen to such things with a cold detachment, because it was not likely they would themselves in person have to spill a victim's blood. This, after all, was normally left to the SS rank and file, the trained killers, men recruited for front-line duties in the so-called Action Groups, or to the labour squads assembled to carry out the extermination routines developed by the technicians of mass-genocide.

The absurd, the trivial, the macabre, the terrible, all make up the SS story, which imposed the ultimate in human suffering on many millions of innocent people. The smiling VIP at a Party reception, dusting his new black uniform as he sips his black-market liquor, stands at one end of the sinister SS spectrum, while at the other, hidden away from public sight, some terrorized woman screams as a man in the same elegant garb hits her across the face. There is polite applause for Himmler, adjusting his rimless pince-nez before addressing the latest conference, while in the confines of some backroom Adolf Eichmann plans the logistics of transportation for the next fifty thousand Jews to be exterminated. The notorious Dr Mengele (the former SS doctor who is still at large in Paraguay) stood in the same black uniform on the receiving ramp at Auschwitz, dictating with a flip of his riding whip who should go to immediate death and who should endure a few more weeks' existence as an SS slave-worker.

All this, and more than this, became the punitive function of the SS, once the Nazis had achieved full power. And behind them, working in close alliance with the SS, were the men and women of the Gestapo, police either in uniform or plain clothes with the special function of maintaining political security in Germany and later in the German-occupied countries. These were the men who came for you in the small hours of the night, their cars, tyres screaming, braking suddenly to a halt in the street below, snatching you, half-awake and terrified, from the arms of your wife and children. They were the specialists in brutal interrogation, with or without their medieval machines of torture, who knew by hard experience the finer limits of human endurance and the stages by which any information they required, true or false, could be most effectively extracted.

Better even than the SS, the Gestapo learnt the melodramatic techniques of terrorization which form an inevitable part in the conduct of a police state. A melodramatic style in terrorization is a psychological factor in conditioning those who must be pursued, harried, and punished. Sheer uncertainty is a further factor; when a person does not know through months or even years what may happen to him from day to day or night to night, powers of resistance in the most resilient can be gradually worn away.

The network of administrative machinery which lay behind this arbitrary form of power grew up largely behind the backs of the German public. They saw it only in its outward manifestations – the undergrowth of published decrees, laws, and regulations which finally hedged them in. Behind the scenes, at the desks of ministries and Party offices, the conspiracy of the bureaucrats had also taken place, created by men with a genius for stopping up the loopholes of civil liberty and the citizen's right of protest. On the whole, the German public took it meekly, with a fatalistic shrug of the shoulders; they saw it as a gradually encroaching *fait accompli*, far too dangerous to resist.

These then were the conditions in Germany, and eventually in the occupied territories of Europe, which began in 1933 and lasted until the final defeat of Hitler brought liberation for the living. Some two-thirds of Europe became subject to this organized form of tyranny.

It happened in our century, and judgment on those involved in the worst excesses of the SS is still being reached in West Germany, and will continue to be in the years ahead. How did this tragedy in Europe come about? And who were the men who planned it?

Heinrich Himmler and the rudimentary SS

Himmler was born in 1900. His father was a respected man, a devout Catholic and a schoolmaster who had at one time been the private tutor of Prince Heinrich of Bavaria, after whom he had named his son. Young Heinrich was still a schoolboy when the First World War began, but he was just old enough to have qualified as an officer cadet in 1918 by the time the fighting was all over. His indifferent health did not deter him in his obsessive ambition to undertake a military career, while his enthusiastic nationalism had been developing strongly during his wartime schooldays.

Once the war was over and lost, Himmler was forced to suppress for a while his ambitions to wear uniform, and he turned to the study of agriculture. Naturally, he required little urging to join the new Nazi Party, since it was a right-wing nationalistic movement suited to his outlook. He joined in 1923, just in time to pose for a photograph which still survives and shows him standing, solemn and upright, clutching a standard while taking part in Hitler's

abortive Munich *Putsch*, which led the following year to the future Führer's ten-month confinement in Landsberg Castle. It also meant the brief imprisonment of the man whose flag young Himmler had been holding. This was the notorious Ernst Röhm, head of Hitler's brownshirt movement, the SA (*Sturmabteilungen* or Assault Sections) – the supporters of the Nazi Party who paraded arrogantly in the streets and were eventually to terrorize the law-abiding German public. Röhm, however, gave up his position as SA leader in 1925, and became a military adviser in Bolivia.

Himmler was given a minor post on the staff of the brothers Gregor and Otto Strasser, who took charge of the Party's interests in Hitler's absence and who were, on his release, to become for a while his apparent rivals for the leadership in the movement. Himmler, then aged twenty-four, earned the modest wage of 120 marks a month, the equivalent of some $30 in the values of the period. Hitler's intensive campaign for power began in 1925, after his release

The failed intellectual. Joseph Goebbels, the Nazi propaganda chief

was to parade with speakers at Nazi public rallies and take immediate counteraction if there were any show of violence. The SS had been formed originally as early as 1922 before the Munich *Putsch*; their duty then was confined to taking care of Hitler. Reformed in 1925 as the Protection Squads, they had the following year received a special 'blood-banner' from Hitler's hands for their 'gallant' services at Munich in 1923.

Himmler was not expected to live on his diminutive salary, and his work was for a while considered as part-time. His needs, however, were very modest, and in 1927 he married a nurse from Berlin, a woman seven years older than himself. Between them, they acquired a smallholding in the countryside near Munich, though Himmler gave less and less time to this as his SS duties developed. Then in 1929, at the age of only twenty-eight, he achieved full command of the SS. He was given the grand title of *Reichsführer SS*, a rank he held to the end of his life and one which was to make him the most feared man in the whole of German-occupied Europe.

The SS at this time was, in fact, little more than a platoon which, despite its special duties, was subordinate to the SA. Himmler had only about 200 men at his disposal. It must be understood that, in spite of his military ambitions, Himmler was essentially a desk-worker. He was a man of restricted, yet persistent ability, with a passion for administrative detail, and an inordinate personal ambition bred in him since childhood. His poor sight, his weak stomach, his thin and ailing body scarcely marked him out as a man of action; nor had he, like Goebbels, any pretensions to be called an intellectual. He was, rather, a petty bureaucrat, but with the difference that he had the stamina to push himself through to the top by virtue of his evident loyalty, his fervid nationalism and racial pride, and his capacity to sacrifice everything in the face of hard work. He gave himself completely to the cause of Nazism; his belief in it was never that of a cynical opportunist, such as Goebbels, but that of a quiet and patient fanatic who never sought the lime-

from prison. Having learned from hard experience that it might not pay to use illegal methods, he was now determined to get his way by using so-called legitimate means – that is, by fighting every election and winning a majority, if he could, in the *Reichstag* and the state parliaments. The Party's agents had been placed on a more professional basis, and able men were beginning to be recruited. Joseph Goebbels, a brilliant young agitator who was making a name for himself as an effective platform orator and spokesman for the Party, was sent in 1926 to 'conquer' Berlin, the 'Red city' as it was called, because of the strong left-wing movement to be found there. Goebbels, small, club-footed, sharp-tongued, and fearlessly insolent where authority was concerned, proved oustandingly successful in Berlin, and soon became the Party's campaign manager in fighting the numerous elections during the next few years. So, in 1928, the Party achieved its first success by winning twelve seats in the *Reichstag*. Among those chosen to occupy them were both Goebbels and Hermann Göring.

It was in 1926 that Himmler had met with his first reward; he was appointed deputy-leader of the Protection Units (*Schutzstaffeln*, or SS), the bodyguards whose original task

light but was always ready when he was wanted.

The principal cast for Hitler's drama was assembling. The outstanding personalities before 1930 did not include Himmler, who was never a man to shine on the speaker's rostrum. Rather, he was a Machiavellian figure; his voice was best expressed in memoranda, but his ears were in every room. Soon, in the early 1930s, he was to count for more. The men with the prominent speaking parts were, first, Gregor Strasser, Himmler's initial employer, now Party leader in the north, a man with socialist rather than right-wing leanings who for a brief while bid fair to rival Hitler for the national Party leadership. Secondly, there was Hermann Göring, the former air-ace who had marched with Hitler in 1923 at Munich but had fled the country with his Swedish wife when the Munich *Putsch* had failed. He was badly wounded, and his drug addiction stemmed from the seda-

The war hero. Hermann Göring with Himmler (right)

tives he was given. Göring had with some difficulty reinstated himself with Hitler when he returned from Sweden in 1928 after undergoing a temporary cure for the drug addiction. Thirdly, there was, somewhat later, Ernst Röhm whom Hitler invited to return from Bolivia and take up his old command of the SA. Röhm, though a notorious homosexual, was an able commander; the increasing army of brownshirts, who were to be Hitler's shock-troops when the crucial elections were being fought, needed firm control, since the campaigns were to be conducted with street battles and the baser forms of violence. Among the supporting players in Hitler's political melodrama were such men as Rudolf Hess, Hitler's close friend and amanuensis when he had composed his 'prophetic' book, *Mein Kampf*, during 1924 in Landsberg

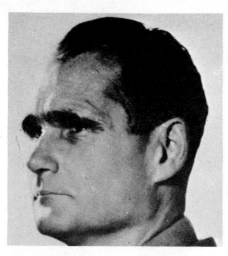

The Führer's faithful lieutenant:
Rudolf Hess

Specialist in anti-Jewish propaganda:
Julius Streicher

Castle, Julius Streicher, the virulent anti-Semite and collector of pornographic documents, which constituted his alleged 'evidence' against Jewish morals, and the so-called philosopher of the movement, Alfred Rosenberg, author of *The Myth of the Twentieth Century* (1930), in whose mind simmered the half-baked theories of 'Aryan' supremacy inherited from 19th Century 'Social-Darwinist' thinking in Germany on selective breeding and the like. The ideas of Rosenberg and his disciple, Walter Darré, formed the 'philosophical' basis for Himmler's dreams of turning the SS into an elite movement demonstrating the racial 'purity' of the world's most powerful *Herrenvolk*.

But this odd cast of players would have stood for nothing had not Hitler emerged as the star that guided them, the sun round which, as planets, they revolved. From January 1925 to January 1933 Hitler's conspiracy for power assumed a gathering momentum, and by the end of the month the Nazi Party recently re-established with a skeleton staff and seriously divided swung up into the saddle after a bare eight years of energetic striving for the mastery of Germany's political machine.

This could only have happened when a man of unique force encounters circumstances uniquely biassed in his favour. In a society seething with

resentment at the outcome of the war, the slogans of the Nazi platform offered a ready panacea for the ills of a Germany which, they claimed, had been largely self-defeated and betrayed. Men with neither work nor purpose responded to the violent cameraderie of a fighting clan. The clashes on the streets gave full rein to repressions in the mob, while Party meetings turned to rallies conducted with all the artificial fervour of some emotional crusade. What these men most needed were some scapegoats on whom to turn and vent their spleen; Hitler gave them these objectives – here the Jews, there the Communists or Social Democrats. He attacked the obvious weakness and shortcomings of a Republic insecurely struggling towards becoming a parliamentary democracy without a united country behind its back.

The old right-wing nationalists and military cliques were still a force in German politics. The system of proportional representation meant that each faction could place its delegates in the seats of government at both the state and federal levels. Weakened by division at the top, the government became an easy target for Hitler's vituperative tongue. It became for him the humiliating symbol of the Treaty of Versailles, of the shame of reparations, of servility before the Allies, of the 'stab in the back' that had dishonoured and disarmed Germany's 'undefeated' armies in 1918, and of the loss of Germany's colonial empire. In a nation full of men marching for varied causes in the flood of private armies, it was not difficult for the Nazi Party to find a place to sink its roots.

For Hitler, the only morality that counted was dedication to his cause. He had proclaimed this without shame in the pages of *Mein Kampf*, in which the goals of Nazism were set down in prose which is virtually unreadable, and which to some extent obscured the true intention that its meanderings implied. For example, Hitler wrote: 'The majority can never replace the man; the majority represents not only ignorance but also cowardice... The Jew lives as a parasite thriving on the substance of other nations... In standing guard against the Jew I am defending the handiwork of God... Every manifestation of human culture, every product of art, science and technical skill, is almost exclusively the product of Aryan creative power. It was the Aryan alone who founded a superior type of humanity; therefore he represents the archetype of what we understand by the term: Man... The greatness of the Aryan is not based on his intellectual powers, but rather on his willingness to devote all his faculties to the service of the community. Here the instinct for self-preservation has reached its noblest form... Never consider the Reich secure unless, for centuries to come, it is in a position to give every descendant of our race a piece of ground and soil that he can call his own. Never forget that the most sacred of all rights in this world is man's right to the earth which he wants to cultivate for himself and that the holiest of all sacrifices is that of the blood poured out for it... The strongest will be destined to fulfil the great mission . . . The whole system of education and training will be directed towards fostering in the child the conviction that he is unquestionably a match for any and everybody... A State which, in an epoch of racial adulteration, devotes itself to the duty of preserving the best elements of its racial stock must one day become master of the Earth.'

Himmler lapped all this up. Already he had dreams of making his minute force a knightly order giving contemporary reality to an old Teutonic myth. He played no extraordinary part in the ceaseless political campaigning which led finally to Hitler becoming Chancellor, although in 1930 he became one of the Party members with a seat in the *Reichstag*. He was fully occupied in gradually building up the strength of the SS forces; with only some 400 in 1931, plus 1,500 part-time recruits, it had reached some 30,000 by 1932, and the following year over 50,000. However, the SS still remained nominally part of the SA, both forces being dependent on the growing millions of unemployed in Germany.

Along with his friend Walter Darré, a former civil servant who later became Hitler's Minister of Agriculture, Himmler devised an extraordinary marriage code for his men. Darré, author in 1929 of a book called *Blood and Soil*, converted Himmler to the 'religion of the blood', an insidious revival of pagan superstitition in the 'strong peasant', the man of racial purity, the blond saviour of superior humanity from degrading infiltration by the 'lower' races, which began with the Jews and Slavs because they were widespread in Europe and had already grievously 'lowered' the shining German stock through their interbreeding. With 'purity' went also the doctrine of the ruthless. 'A culture always decays.' Darré's master, Rosenberg, had written, 'when humanitarian ideals . . . obstruct the right of the dominant race to rule those it has subjugated.'

In 1931 Darré joined SS headquarters, such as it then was, to organize the all-important Race and Settlement Office *(Rasse und Siedlungshauptamt)*. This new department had been formed to prescribe the racial standards which the SS should henceforth observe, and the methods of tracing the 'pure' descent of those responsible for maintaining the SS as representatives of the so-called 'Aryan' stock. This favoured the blond against the dark, the Germanic against the Slav or Latin, and

The abortive putsch of 1923. *Above left:* Hossbach, leader of the Munich SA, and some of his men before the coup. *Above right:* Himmler holds a standard at a barricade. *Below:* After the refounding of the NSDAP, Hitler conducts a party meeting. (Rosenberg, left with hands clasped, Strasser and Himmler right)

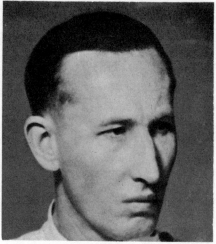

Left: the Nazi race ideologue: Walther Darré. Right: The cashiered naval officer: Reinhard Heydrich, Himmler's brutal deputy. Far right: Men of the SA set out on a propaganda parade in 1929

resulted in the SS marriage 'law' of December 1931, of which the following are the crucial clauses:

'Every SS man who aims to get married must procure for this purpose the marriage certificate of the Reichsführer SS.'

'SS members who though denied marriage certificates marry in spite of this, will be removed from the SS.'

'The working-out of the details of marriage petitions is the task of the Race Office of the SS.'

'The Race Office of the SS directs the SS Clan Book, in which the families of SS members will be entered after the marriage certificate is issued.'

Every member of the SS had from 1932 to carry his Clan Book (Sippenbuch) and obtain a certificate of approval for any girl he chose to marry. Thus, Darré's office kept 'stud' records for every SS man, whose 'Aryan' blood had to be proved uncontaminated as far back as 1750. Elaborate forms were devised for carrying out this process, and as the years went by and the SS grew in numbers, the research staff increased proportionally in order to carry out these laborious researches. Even in the years of war, when Himmler was carrying the heaviest burdens, he would still pause to ponder over some individual's genealogical table.

It became a fetish.

Needless to say, the thing was nonsense, and more honoured in the breach than the observance. If an SS man made a girl pregnant he more often than not got away with marriage also. And there was ample opportunity for faking when it came to one's ancestors as far back as the 18th Century. What made nonsense of the 'law' from the start was not only the pernicious racial premises on which it was established, but the corruption it invited in the hands of those who conducted the detailed administration. Lip-service had to be paid to Himmler, but the *Sippenbuch* soon survived only as a sick joke. From the point of view of the world outside, Hitler's regime later came to be identified with the blond, blue-eyed youths and the flaxen-haired, firm-breasted girls whose torsos glistened in the illustrated journals and filled the screens in the Nazi war films and propaganda newsreels.

Himmler scarcely qualified physically for the ideal standards he had set up for others. But in June 1931, he recruited a young man who in every respect satisfied his needs. This was Reinhard Heydrich, a former naval lieutenant of good family who had recently been dismissed because he had seduced and jilted the daughter

of a prominent industrialist who had the ear of Grand Admiral Raeder. Yet from Himmler's point of view, Heydrich appeared ideal; he was tall and handsome, with a brilliant intellect. Heydrich was outstanding as a violinist, as a linguist, and as a sportsman – an expert fencer and skier. He also had a virile taste for girls. He qualified politically, because at the early age of sixteen he had joined the Free Corps movement, the right-wing nationalist freebooters dedicated to soldiering, who had maintained their own idea of German law and order during the difficult, post-war years. As a lapsed Catholic he was happy to take Himmler's pagan rituals in his stride, though he thought them entirely ludicrous. Himmler made him chief of the newly-formed SS Intelligence Service, the *Sicherheitsdienst* or SD, which Heydrich rapidly developed into a highly organized spy-ring, a secret service which kept useful files on everyone whose record could be of value. He became Himmler's right-hand man, counteracting with his ruthless energy his chief's chronic diffidence when it came to making hard or difficult decisions.

Himmler by 1932 was still a shadowy figure. Few outside the SS and the higher ranks of the Party really knew him. Though never to be well-off, Himmler was now more comfortably placed financially, with his Party salary increased, his allowance as a *Reichstag* deputy – which also gave him free travel throughout the country – and his small-holding in Waltrudering, which helped maintain his wife and infant daughter, to whom he was devoted. The image he created was that of the loyal, dutiful Party man, hiding behind his pince-nez and his slightly obseqious but knowing smirk. Few saw in him anything really formidable – he was merely the rather over-titled *Reichsführer SS*, the man with the odd ideas about racial 'purity' which were always good for a hearty laugh. He did not aspire to join Hitler's inner circle of confidants in the manner of Göring and Goebbels, always vying with each other to gain the greater influence with the Führer. Like the rest of the Party men, he did not take his position in the *Reichstag* very seriously; they occupied their seats merely as a temporary expedient in the conspiracy to capture the State. It suited Himmler at this stage to limit himself; it was enough if he were seen to be loyal and hard-working, but no more. He regarded himself, rather, as a future spiritual leader, almost a prophet, with the SS as his disciples.

Round-shouldered and demure, Himmler stands with Röhm and their allied nationalist henchmen at a Harzburg Front rally in 1931

Establishing the police state

Hitler's crucial steps to power during 1932 are well enough known – the violent confrontation with the German Communists, the winning of support alike from certain industrialists and the nationalist-minded unemployed, the brilliant propaganda campaigns to win votes at the elections, and the rise in voting strength at the polls from 6,409,600 votes in 1930 (as against under a million in 1928) to 13,745,000 in July 1932, about one-third of the electorate. Through various back-stage intrigues, President Hindenburg was manoeuvred into offering his one-time corporal the Chancellorship in January 1933, and, glowing with his triumph, Hitler reached out and took it.

In all this the SS had played no special part which can be considered separate from that of the SA as a whole. Himmler was still technically subordinate to Röhm, but in Hitler's tortuous mind the policy of divide and rule always seemed to make good sense; it was a form of security, or appeared to be so. The greatly inflated ranks of the SA – some 100,000 men by 1930, rising to around three million by 1933–34 – were necessary at this stage to give the Party its shock-troops among the voters and to put up a formidable front against the Communists on the streets. Here the Communists (some four and a half million strong in the 1930 polls) were constantly incited to give battle, in order to prove to the prosperous industrialists of the Right, Hitler's principal source of finance, that a strong, nationalist leader was necessary to bring the Left to heel and keep the land safe for big business to prosper in. After all, Germany was to become the 'bulwark against Communism'.

But Hitler was well aware of the danger he was in from his own SA forces. They could only too easily grow out of hand. For this reason he liked to think of the existence of a second, specially loyal force within the force; it was, after all, Hitler himself who had originally instructed Himmler to develop the SS as an elite with their own *esprit de corps*. So long

Kurt Daluege (right), Himmler and Röhm on the rostrum at a Berlin stadium in 1933. In the foreground: Prince Waldeck (right), and Sepp Dietrich (third from right)

as the SS remained a minor, specialist force for the purpose of guarding the platform at rallies and meetings, it had little use as a counter-measure against any faction in the SA which needed disciplining. The first disciplinary act of the SS against a rebellious SA faction had taken place in Berlin during 1930–31 on Hitler's express order.

However, when Röhm had returned as SA commandant in 1931, he had renewed his friendship (if that is the term for it) with Himmler, and until 1933 they virtually worked together. But Röhm's period of power was to be relatively short-lived; in little more than three years after his return from Bolivia he would be dead, executed on Hitler's orders. Meanwhile, the unstable Weimar government had been unable to stand any more of these para-military parades and struggles in the streets; in April 1932 both the SA and the SS had been officially disbanded by government order. This order had held good until July of the same year, when Schleicher, the new Chancellor, had rescinded it.

Himmler did not want the SS to degenerate into a rabble of street hooligans along the lines of the SA, whose terrorist activities were jeopardizing Hitler's support from the industrialists. All the greater reason, therefore, for establishing special training and disciplinary codes for the SS, and the SD under Heydrich, on the strength of whose growing dossiers dangerous men could be sprung upon and charged with their delinquencies. The work of Heydrich was the first element in SS organisation which pointed ahead to the future police state. On the other hand, the SS was already being used as a force to establish social prestige for the Nazis. It became the policy even before 1933 to encourage princes, aristocrats, retired generals, and even church dignitaries to accept honorary rank in the SS. Some of these were named when evidence was being given before the International Military Tribunal at Nuremberg after the war – they included, for example, Prince Waldeck, the Prince von Mecklenburg, the General Graf von der Schulenburg, and the Archbishop of Brunswick.

Himmler and Heydrich, along with the other Nazi leaders, were ready for action the moment Hitler became Chancellor on 30th January 1933. It is an error to assume that the Nazi Party came to full power by this single accession to office – it was merely a prime stage in the conspiracy to achieve it. Much more hard work, both on stage and behind the scenes, had to be done, most of it against time, before the Enabling Act of 23rd March was passed in the *Reichstag*, giving Hitler his dictatorial rights. The Nazis, now the single largest Party in the *Reichstag*, did not command an absolute majority in the House, though Göring remained the elected President. It was necessary for immediate, planned action to take place. The outcome was a brilliant piece of strategy in which Göring, not Himmler at this stage, played the principal role.

The balance of power in the Cabinet appeared to put the Nazi leaders at a disadvantage. The bargaining with President Hindenburg and the leaders of the other Parties in the *Reichstag* led to a three-to-one majority against the new Chancellor – three Nazis to nine old-time politicians. Franz von Papen, the right-wing Vice-Chancellor, believed that this would be more than sufficient to curb Hitler, but he accepted Göring, one of the other Nazi members of the Cabinet, as Minister of the Interior for the state of Prussia, of which Papen himself was Reich Commissioner, or head of state. It was this office held by Göring which gave the Nazis control of the thin end of the wedge for establishing their police state. Prussia was by far the largest state in Germany, including in its boundaries the capital, Berlin, and important industrial centres. Meanwhile Göring, President of the *Reichstag*, dissolved the House the day after Hitler's assumption of office, since it was realised there was no chance of agreement between the Nazis and their principal rivals. New elections were set for 5th March, five weeks ahead. Goebbels then, as election campaign manager, set out to achieve what he called 'a masterpiece of propaganda' in order to ensure an absolute victory. In this, as we shall see, he was to fail.

Hitler with President von Hindenburg

Göring then divided his time between the vital business of the election and setting up the first stages of a police state in Prussia, where the regional parliament was also dissolved on 4th February. Writing only the following year in his brief book, *Germany Reborn*, addressed specially to Great Britain, Göring said: 'To begin with, it seemed to me of the first importance to get the weapon of the police firmly into my own hands. Here it was that I made the first sweeping changes. Out of 32 police chiefs I removed 22. Hundreds of inspectors and thousands of police sergeants followed in the course of the next month. New men were brought in, and in every case these men came from the great reservoir of the storm-troopers and the Guards.' 'Göring is cleaning out the Augean stables', laughed Goebbels to himself in the private diary he was keeping to record the events of these most stirring times.

It is a curiosity of Nazi history that it was Göring, and not Himmler, who created the first Nazi political police, an initial unit of the Gestapo, and the first official Nazi concentration camps. Quite independently of Himmler, he placed the Berlin SS leader, Kurt Daluege (who had once been a refuse disposal officer, but was now an SS general) in charge of the new Prus-

sian police force, and Rudolf Diels, who had married Göring's cousin, Ilse, in charge of Berlin Police Bureau I A, the state political police, which was later to become the Gestapo. In this he was assisted by the prior existence of political police in Berlin under the Weimar constitution, as a defence against the post-war anarchy and extremists of the Right and Left. Most of the men involved proved ready recruits for Göring's new establishment, including Diels himself, who had been in charge of the state political police before Göring's administration.

Most of the rank and file of the career police were ready to work for the Nazis; they did not want to join the ranks of the unemployed. Then Göring, in the name of state security at a time of emergency he had largely created himself (a typical Nazi ploy), armed his regular police, and on 22nd February supplemented them with 25,000 SA men and 10,000 from the SS. 'A bullet fired from the barrel of a police pistol is my bullet,' he declared. Their wage was three marks daily, and they had free transport. For the rest, they lived on plunder.

That great sign of emergency, the *Reichstag* fire, which blazed so mysteriously on the night of 27th February, was almost certainly an act initiated by the Nazis themselves. The final,

27

conclusive evidence for this is lacking, and arguments for and against Nazi involvement are still raised from time to time. Whether Nazi collaborators set fire to the *Reichstag* or not, neither Hitler nor Göring hesitated. This was proclaimed a Communist plot to take over the state, and they forthwith set the armed police and their auxiliaries from the SA and the SS onto the Communists, who included many of former *Reichstag* deputies. It was a fine opportunity to suppress their rivals prior to the elections a few days hence. In all some 5,000 people were arrested in Berlin alone. In addition, the rallies of the Social Democrats and the Catholic Centre Party were constantly broken up, and in February alone over fifty men prominent among the opposition died from acts of violence. On 29th February, normal civil liberties guaranteed by the Constitution were suspended, which meant that anyone could be arrested and detained without trial.

On 5th March, when the last, so-called 'free' elections for the *Reichstag* finally took place, the Nazi Party, in spite of its vicious efforts to intimidate the electorate, polled only forty-four per cent of the votes cast, and so failed to gain the absolute majority Hitler technically needed. But by now it scarcely mattered, with the Communist deputies gone. The notorious Enabling Act of 23rd March was passed without major difficulty; only the Social Democrats were left to vote against the bill. Hitler by this act was given the power to govern by emergency decree. The dictatorship had begun.

It was in March that Göring first established concentration camps in Prussia on behalf of the regime. He always liked to claim that he had adopted the idea from Great Britain, and that it was British forces in South Africa who had made use of concentration camps during the Boer War.

Below: Hitler poses with his 'comrades in the struggle' the night before taking power, 30th January, 1933. *Right to left:* Hess, Himmler, Darré, Göring, Röhm, Hitler, Goebbels, Frick. *Right:* A month later, the Reichstag burns

Communists are arrested by an 'auxiliary policeman' in 1933

He also liked to claim that these *Konzentrationslager* were really centres for political rehabilitation, and that any brutalities which took place were strictly against his will. Giving his testimony at Nuremberg in 1946, he said: 'Of course I gave instructions that such things should not happen. That they did happen and happened everywhere to a smaller or greater extent I have just stated. I always stressed that these things should not happen, because it was important to me to win over some of these people for our side and to re-educate them.' He even admitted knowledge of other camps set up in the provinces during the early period by other Nazi officials. It was here, he claimed, that the real cruelties took place, and as soon as he knew of the existence of these camps he had them closed down.

On 26th April Göring moved the Prussian political police to its own headquarters at 8 Prinz-Albrecht-Strasse, a name later to become infamous as the Nazi prison for political detainees and a centre for the worst treatment of victims undergoing interrogation. In June, the force was officially renamed the *Geheime Staatspolizei*, the Secret State Police, or Gestapo. Göring, like Himmler, had at this time a vision of himself as head of a unified German political police force, and he was quite open about the need for freedom to arrest his opponents.

Meanwhile Himmler, deprived for a while of the power he most coveted, had to give ground before Göring's ruthless energy and the independent police venture for the moment controlled by Daluege and Diels in Germany's largest state. Hitler had appointed Himmler President of Police in Munich, a very secondary post, certainly, but one upon which he could nevertheless begin to capitalize. Using Heydrich's dossiers, Himmler rapidly purged the police at

Roll call for political prisoners in Sachsenhausen concentration camp August, 1933

hand following the pattern set by Göring. Munich, like Berlin, already had its political police force, and many of these men were ready to serve the new masters. Among them was Heinrich Müller, later to head the Gestapo.

Between April 1933 and the same month in 1934, when Himmler was finally successful in becoming head of a unified political police force in Germany, through Hitler he furthered his own interests by gradually acquiring control of the political police in a succession of German states other than Göring's Prussia – Bavaria in April, Hamburg in October, and in Mecklenburg, Lübeck, Württemberg, Baden, Hesse, Thüringen, and Anhalt in December. In January 1934, he took over the same office in Oldenburg, Bremen, and Saxony.

He had also established his own 'model' concentration camp at Dachau, twelve miles from Munich. This was in March 1933; Himmler's

brief order for 'protective custody' ran as follows: 'Based on Article I of the Decree of the Reich President for the Protection of People and State of February 28th 1933, you are taken into protective custody in the interest of public security and order. Reason: suspicion of activities inimical to the State.' Precise and orderly, Himmler drew up the most careful regulations for the discipline of the camp, in which there already appears that most insidious form of terrorisation, the deliberate use of rumour inspired by fear: The term commitment to a concentration camp is to be openly announced as "until further notice".... In certain cases the Reichsführer SS and Chief of the German Police will order flogging in addition to detention in a concentration camp.... In this case, too, there is no objection to spreading the rumour of this increased punishment ... to add to the deterrent effect. Naturally, particu-

larly suitable and reliable people are to be chosen for spreading such news. The following offenders, considered as agitators, will be hanged: anyone who . . . makes inciting speeches and holds meetings, forms cliques, loiters around with others; who for the purpose of supplying the propaganda of the opposition with atrocity stories, collects true or false information about the concentration camp.'

After Hitler's Enabling Act of March 1933, the first phase of a reign of terror began. But there was trouble in the ranks of the Nazis themselves, the trouble between the rival concentration camps to which Göring was to refer at Nuremberg, for instance. But over and above this, the SA, Röhm's unruly hordes of unemployed Nazi brownshirts, were clamouring for reward and for revenge on their opponents now the Führer was in power. The SA constituted a grave threat to Hitler's own authority now he was in the Chancellery and needed to gain the confidence of the 'top' people in the army, banks and industry. In other words, the bravos of the streets whose clamour had hustled him to power had now to be called to order and, if necessary, disbanded. .

Göring, volatile by nature and never free from the influence of his drugs, could be indolent at one moment and energetic at the next. Once Hitler's authority seemed secure, his restless interests turned to other, multifarious duties, including his interests in the Luftwaffe. He was to become the collector of many diverse functions, in order to boost his thriving ego. His celebrated 'good humour' and his craving for popularity must have warned him that the office of head of the secret political police would scarcely stand him in good stead. It did not take much coaxing by the Führer to persuade him to hand this unpleasant office to the man who was pressing Hitler to unify the political police under a single, national authority, controlled by himself, *Reichsführer SS* Heinrich Himmler. 'When the Führer asked me

Temporarily eclipsed by Göring, Himmler eventually won control of the Gestapo

to do this and said it would be the correct thing and that it was proved necessary that the enemies of the State be fought throughout the Reich in a uniform way, I actually handed the police over to Himmler,' Göring stated on the stand at Nuremberg. Himmler took over the Prussian Gestapo on 20th April 1934, with Heydrich as his deputy. However, it was not until 1936 that Himmler was confirmed by Hitler as official Chief of the German Police as a whole, and given ministerial rank.

But there was another pressing reason why Göring should placate this earnest rival, and make of him an ally. Röhm, dangerous and restive, had been given a seat in the Cabinet in December 1933. It was part of Hitler's wary nature, his intuitive self-protection, to keep his colleagues guessing by making such arbitrary awards. Promotions, given suddenly and without consultation, administered psychological shocks to those who liked to think, as Göring always did, that they were Hitler's chosen favourites. Göring called himself Hitler's 'Paladin', and believed he was his chosen deputy. So he traded his Prussian Gestapo for a sound alliance with an up-and-coming man, who took his tasks so seriously and stood so well in Hitler's favour.

The next event in the unwritten schedule was to rid Germany of Röhm, whose SA forces were estimated to number some three million, a huge and wholly unofficial army. This would be easier now, with Himmler's well-stocked SS and Heydrich's secret dossiers on Röhm and his male consorts. Himmler had moved his headquarters to Berlin, and together with Göring he set about working on Hitler's stubborn will. The Führer, elated by his extraordinary good fortune, basked in one of his more conservative moods. He did not want to wash the Party's dirty linen under the still powerful eyes of Germany's 'establishment'. His head was full of plans for further consolidation in his power. Hindenburg still held the Presidency, but he was aged and infirm: Hitler had it in mind to succeed him, once he had died a natural death. Röhm, however, tipped the scales against himself by openly proposing

33

**The Anschluss of Austria, March, 1938.
The Führer returns in triumph to Vienna**

in the Cabinet that the SA be merged
with the German army with Röhm
(or so he hinted) in command. Hitler
knew as well as anyone that this was
dangerous and stupid talk.

The one, powerful force in the State
which Hitler had not yet conquered
was the army. The Army High Command (OKH) was nationalist and right-
wing, but there were naturally many
among the generals who looked
askance at the Austrian corporal who
had climbed the political path to
power. Like the industrialists, they
had only tolerated this awkward, ill-
bred, unaccountable man because he
was so firmly opposed to the common
enemy – the solid Communist bloc.
Like the President and the politicians,
they had thought they could easily

'use' him once they allowed him to
become the Chancellor.

Hitler, knowing his men, adapted
the guise of conservative respect-
ability in order to bargain with OKH.
The politicians he could now afford
to disregard, but not the industrialists
or the generals. The Nazi talk at the
top was all for order, discipline, and
progress for the State. The only major
embarrassment left to Hitler among
his own adherents was the Brownshirts who, with little left to do, made
the streets unruly and frightened the
substantial middle-of-the-road bour-
geois of whose moral support he now
stood most in need – not merely in
Germany, but in the eyes of the
Western world, more especially Great
Britain, France and that distant
place he knew so little about, the
United States. When Sir John Simon
and Anthony Eden paid a formal visit

to Germany in February 1934, they found Hitler quiet and amenable, and even ready with an offer to demobilize two-thirds of his SA.

With a typically sudden gesture, Hitler yielded to the pressure of his advisers. Röhm must go, and with him the SA. Heydrich's SD files were drained for evidence against him, and against some hundreds of others, high and low, suspected of disloyalty. The SD was now officially recognised by Hitler as the Party's intelligence service from which no information could be withheld. The Brownshirts were put on a month's official leave, and Röhm retired sick to Bavaria, accompanied by his boys. Himmler, conscious of what was coming, toured his principal SS regional establishments to reinforce the importance of their loyalty to Hitler. This was in readiness for the secret report at the end of June that Röhm and many others were planning a *coup d'etat*.

The blow was struck at dawn on 30th June 1934, and it was struck by the SS with Hitler at their head. The Führer flew to Munich overnight and drove in a cavalcade of cars to the sanatorium at Tegernsee where Röhm lay still asleep. He was hauled from his bed, bundled into a car, and hurried back to Munich. Hitler, angry and embarrassed by the confrontation, left the dirty business of interrogation and execution to his agents. There was a certain degree of confusion as between the authorities responsible. Röhm was not shot until 2nd July in Munich, after the Nazi field-day had taken place in Berlin. This was the so-called 'Night of the Long Knives'. Here Göring and Himmler between them started the round of slaughter. Prisoners were brought in

The occupation of the Sudetenland, October, 1938. *Above:* Girl greets the Führer *Right:* Entry into Karlsbad

from everywhere to Göring's private residence; their names were checked against a lengthy list which had been typed out for Heydrich, and, if identities tallied, the victims were taken out and shot. The ticking and the shooting went on all night, until Göring called a halt. Among the hundreds who died, shot in Berlin and elsewhere, was Schleicher, a former Chancellor. Papen, the unwanted Vice-Chancellor, only escaped with his life because of Göring's intercession. To kill the current Vice-Chancellor would certainly not look good. Hitler, meanwhile, to show that all was well again, held a garden party in the grounds of his Chancellery. Göring was careful to see that Hindenburg sent him a personal message of congratulation on the total action, though the President himself was lying on his deathbed. When he died on 2nd August, a month after the massacre, Hitler merged the office of Chancellor and President, and officially proclaimed himself the Führer, the Supreme Head of State, as well as Commander-in-Chief of the Armed Forces of the Reich. A personal

oath of loyalty was imposed on every man in uniform.

On 20th July the SS was given its official independence from the discredited SA. With Röhm and their leaders gone, the SA now dissappears into the small print of Nazi history. The SS was left supreme as the force which exercised political discipline on behalf of Hitler and the Party; the SD remained its secret intelligence service, and the Gestapo its investigators, ready to act at a moment's notice and to conduct interrogations under the worst duress.

These were the fruits of eighteen months in office. The police state had been achieved. Hitler, secure now in his own nation, began to turn his attention to others. Home affairs and security were left increasingly to his ministers – especially to Göring and Goebbels, and to Himmler, as *Reichsführer SS* and *de facto* head of the police. During the next five years, 1934-39, the sphere of Nazi power widened – in 1935 the Versailles Treaty was flouted, and universal conscription ordered, in 1936 the demilitarized Rhineland was occupied and the Rome-Berlin axis proclaimed, while in 1938 Austria was annexed (the *Anschluss*), and the pressures on Czechoslovakia and Poland begun.

Pre-war consolidation

Given full, nation-wide control of the secret police, Himmler felt free to conduct his own form of purge. During the months of trouble, recruitment to the SS had been too hurried, and the ranks of what Himmler called his 'National Socialist Soldier Order of Nordic Men' contained many specimens unable to pass so stringent a test. During the years 1934-35, some 60,000 of the less suitable men were released from service, leaving the total force at a strength around 200,000. In future, all recruits until the years of war were required to meet the high standards set down for 'Nordic Man'. The SS remained utterly separate from the army, and both their thinking and their training were different. They were, in fact, the heirs of the old, independent, para-military Free Corps bravos, and not of the army, which regarded their existence with scepticism, if not alarm. Their weapons included small-calibre rifles. A considerable proportion of the 200,000 were part-time and earned their living outside the service. The SS, like the army, took a special oath of personal loyalty to Hitler: 'I swear to you, Adolf Hitler, as Führer and Reich Chancellor, loyalty and bravery. I vow to you, and to those you have named to command me, obedience unto death, so help me God.'

An SS leadership school had been founded as early as 1932 at Bad-Tölz in Bavaria. An SS leader was supposed not only to be physically fit, but also a man of quick intelligence. He must, too, be well-educated politically, which meant politically indoctrinated. As well as sport and gymnastics, the training school offered instruction in history, geography, militarism, and racial 'hygiene'. At the back of Himmler's mind lay a vague accumulation of odd theories – his Catholic upbringing (which he now violently rejected) was not lost upon him, and he still respected the discipline exercised by the Jesuits. Now, however, as a pagan whose beliefs were moulded by the ancient pseudo-Teutonic mythology of blood and earth, he was equally influenced by what he favoured in the tradition of the Teutonic Knights.

Himmler's Aryan ideal

To fulfil these medieval ambitions, Himmler refurbished a splendid old castle at Wewelsburg, in a forest area near the historic town of Paderborn in Westphalia. Walter Schellenberg, who was later, on the death of Heydrich, to take control of the SD, describes the nonsense which went on there: 'It was,' he says, 'adapted to serve as a kind of SS monastery . . . . Here the secret Chapter of the Order assembled once a year. Each member had his own armchair with an engraved silver nameplate, and each had to devote himself to a ritual of spiritual exercises aimed mainly at mental concentration . . . The SS organization had been built up by Himmler on the principles of the Order of the Jesuits. The service statutes and spritual exercises prescribed by Ignatius Loyola formed a pattern which Himmler assiduously tried to copy. Absolute obedience was the supreme rule; each and every order had to be accepted without question.'

When Himmler stayed in Wewelsburg he slept in a room named after Heinrich I, Henry the Fowler, the traditional founder-monarch of the German Reich. In the pursuit of racial 'purity', Himmler instituted a research centre called *Ahnenerbe* (Ancestral Heritage) to investigate the origins of the Nordic stock in man and the qualities it possessed which made it superior to all other races in the species.

Heydrich, who held all this to be rubbish, was nevertheless quite happy to go along with Himmler's eccentricities. He, too, wanted a strong, intelligent, ruthless body of men at his disposal. Also, he knew that he was suspected of having a taint of Jewish blood on his mother's side of the family and, true or not, he wanted to show in his attitude to such decadence that he was incapable of backsliding. Heydrich preferred the more contemporary aspects of the SS, and he started the special SS journal, *Das Schwarze Korps (The Black Guards)*

Below: Schloss Wewelsburg. *Right above:* The Leibstandarte SS Adolf Hitler practise the goose-step. *Right below:* SS insignia

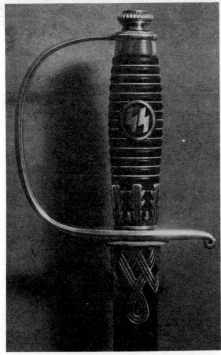

'Harmful elements' at Sachsenhausen in 1939

to help sustain the cameraderie among his men.

Far more deadly than Himmler's play-acting at Wewelsburg were developments in Dachau, the 'model' concentration camp established near to Munich. The first commandant of this punitive centre was SS-Colonel Theodor Eicke, a man who believed whole-heartedly in the efficacy of the harshest discipline. He was a veteran soldier, and for him the only way with men, whether friends or enemies, was ruthless treatment. The training system he instituted started much of the utter brutality and de-humanisation characteristic of the SS. It was he who trained Rudolf Hoess, later to be commandant of Auschwitz, the headquarters of genocide. Hoess joined the SS in 1933, and became an ordinary camp guard under Eicke in 1934. It is commonly thought that the SS

itself, and especially that branch of it which controlled the concentration camps, was deliberately made up of pathological sadists. Whoever chooses to believe this is deluding himself about the baser instincts in ordinary human nature. Fortunately, there are few pronounced psychopaths in human society, and only a small proportion of these would be actually employable as staff. The concentration camps as developed during the war required up to 40,000 SS staff to run them, quite apart from the special, highly-trained interrogators of the SS and Gestapo who worked over their prisoners in such grim places as the prison cells at the Prinz-Albrecht-Strasse.

While it is true that a few camp guards and Gestapo interrogators took continuous, pathological delight in what they were doing, for the most part the men, and eventually the women, in active charge of prisoners were of the kind we might call rather

ordinary, unintelligent men and women in the street. They were, however, chosen because they were tough and insensitive, and they were given a very special training in order to condition them for their work. They were induced to loathe their prisoners and gradually grew accustomed to perform acts of ordinary brutality at their expense. Hoess, in the memoirs he wrote after the war while awaiting trial in a Polish prison, described how he was initiated. The SS staff at Dachau were christened the Death's Head Guards, and they were regularly paraded to witness the savage beatings given to prisoners reminiscent of the floggings administered to disobedient sailors in the Royal Navy during the 18th and early 19th centuries. Camp guards had to accustom themselves to the sight of blood and lacerated flesh as well as to the screams of frightened victims. Prisoners, said Eicke, must always be regarded as hostile, and kept in a state

of absolute subjection. It was the duty of guards to demonstrate their hostility to the prisoners. Eicke instituted a 'cult of severity' and the recognition of the absolute nature of all orders, which had to be carried out unflinchingly. During 1934 Eicke's tenacity met with its reward; Himmler appointed him Inspector of Concentration Camps so that his influence might permeate the total SS punitive system in the camps. Women guards were later to receive their training in the camp at Ravensbrück, which was established just before the war in 1939.

A man trained to scream barbarically during bayonet training is not regarded as a sadist; he is doing his duty. A housewife who swats a fly or crushes a beetle is not regarded as a sadist; she is cleansing her premises. The state of unhygienic degradation in which the SS kept their prisoners was a deliberate policy – not only did it serve to humiliate and subdue them, it also made them appear loathsome in the sight of their guards. They had to be seen to be the human vermin they were claimed to be ideologically. Thus to beat them into subjection, to fell them to the ground, or even to shoot them on the slightest provocation was an act of hygienic self-preservation administered by human beings of racial purity to contaminated sub-humans. According to SS doctrine, this was no act of sadism, but the demonstration of a healthy mind revolted by the creatures who were a poison in the human species. Implicit in the camps from the start was the ultimate crime of genocide.

The SS in its various manifestations attracted every kind of recruit whose blood could be rendered pure enough on paper to satisfy Himmler's searching eye. His desk, weighed down with files relating to the ancestry of the most obscure among his recruits, became a genealogical hotbed. In spite of this racial bottleneck, the SS, duly purged, began to grow again. It attracted a strange and ill-assorted crew. At one end of the scale were the princes and the socialites, the churchmen and the lawyers, the right-wing ex-army officers, the university professors and the doctors; but at the other end were the less elegant

From the start the SS was an élite body, each man in the peak of fitness *(below)* and completely indoctrinated with the Nazi creed *(above)*

barbarians, the shady Free Corps veterans, and even men released from jail for violences committed in the past. The former congregated in their upper-class drawing-rooms and gave the service a seemingly decent, even an intellectual front; the latter volunteered for duty in the concentration camps and kept their identities obscure. In between these 'opposites' there developed a meticulous bureaucracy, representing Himmler's special staff. Among these, for example, was to be that prime administrator, Adolf Eichmann.

SS training from the highest level downwards depended on the two qualities which Himmler constantly discussed and which Heydrich as constantly put into real practice. First came reverence of 'toughness' *(härte)*, toughness towards political opponents and the 'vermin' in the camps. On the other hand, there was the service cameraderie, loyalty to comrades within the SS itself. The SS motto was: 'Honour For Us Means Loyalty'. 'For the SS man there is one absolute principle,' said Himmler, 'he must be honest, decent, loyal, and friendly to persons of our own blood – and to no one else.' Himmler had ordered that cupboards in SS barracks should have no locks or keys on the assumption that SS men were always to be trusted. On other occasions Himmler is recorded as saying: 'This chivalrous attitude must, however, be regarded as lunacy if adopted towards Jews or Bolshevists . . . . True wars, wars between races, are merciless and fought to the last man, until one side or the other is eliminated without trace.' Officers in the SS were therefore as far as possible regarded as the prototypes of toughness; the death of their prisoners was held to be desirable, especially when their numbers increased wholesale in the weeks following Hitler's invasion of Poland.

Let us consider for a few moments certain classes of people who were joining the SS after 1934. Prominent among them were the bright young lawyers, the intellectuals of the movement. Reading law is a standard practice in the German universities for those intending to take up administration, whether in the civil service or in industry. There were many well-

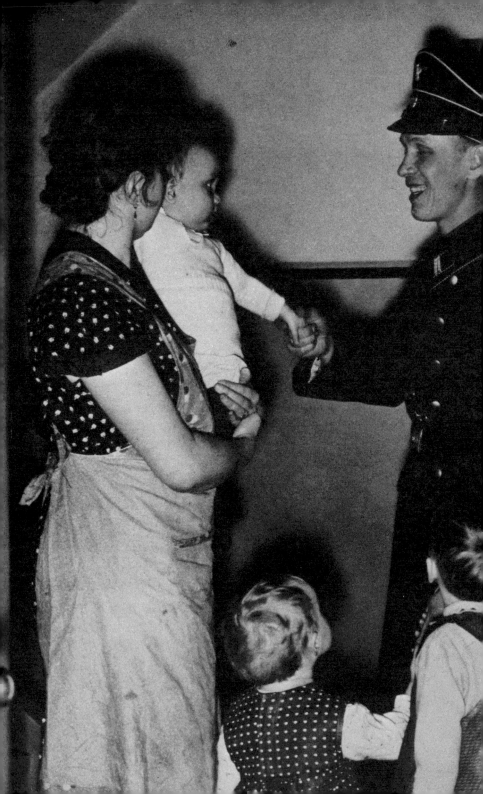

Far left: The good SS man was a devoted husband and father, loyally siring children for the Führer. *Left:* Otto Ohlendorf. *Right:* Walter Schellenburg

qualified young men with right-wing, nationalist sympathies who looked to the new regime for positions offering quick advancement. The headquarters of the SS seemed made for them, with the elegant uniform thrown in. Among the youngest was Walter Schellenberg, whose post-war memoirs were to provide entertaining if fanciful reading about the intrigues within the SS. He was born in 1910. He had studied law and medicine at the university of Bonn, and had joined the SS in 1933 largely because he found there 'the better type of people'. Membership of the SS, he claimed, brought considerable prestige and social advantages, while the beer-hall rowdies of the SA were 'beyond the pale'. After a part-time assignment which he did not like, since it involved route-marches and drill during his free weekends, he was picked out by two SS officers, professors from the university at Bonn – 'one a philologist and the other an educationalist' – who suggested that he accept an 'honorary' assignment to the SD while continuing his legal studies. He was then removed to police headquarters at Frankfurt where he claims that he was used as a spy on the 'highest Party functionaries'. Finally he became a full-time member of staff at Berlin headquarters, working under Heydrich. His description of

Heydrich is a closely-observed portrait: 'He was a tall, impressive figure with a broad, unusually high forehead, small restless eyes as crafty as an animal's and of uncanny power, a long predatory nose, and a wide, full-lipped mouth. His hands were slender and rather too long – they made one think of the legs of a spider. His splendid figure was marred by the breadth of his hips, a disturbingly feminine effect which made him appear even more sinister. His voice was much too high for so large a man and his speech was nervous and staccato . . . The development of a whole nation was guided indirectly by his forceful character. He was far superior to all his political colleagues and controlled them as he controlled the vast intelligence machine of the SD . . . Heydrich had an incredibly acute perception of the moral, human, professional, and political weaknesses of others.'

There is an element in Schellenberg's nature which is not at first sight unattractive – his sense of humour, his eager delight in the Bond-like assignments which were to come his way as an intelligence agent, his unsparing portrait of Himmler,dithering with indecision in moments of high crisis. Though Schellenberg was undoubtedly as amoral and as heartless as the rest, his sheer opportunism

47

of nature makes it necessary for him to write as if he had both heart and soul.

Rather more sinister among the SS intellectuals was Professor Otto Ohlendorf. Born in Hanover in 1907, he became a student of economics, philosophy, and sociology, and later a doctor of jurisprudence. Ohlendorf joined the SD in 1936 at the age of twenty-nine, and he was given charge of certain cultural, economic, and legal matters at headquarters. He was to survive the war and give important evidence at Nuremberg before being put on trial himself as a mass-murderer, as we shall see. Several of these intellectuals became efficient killers, though Schellenberg was not among them. The university men proved self-disciplined and ruthless, and precise in their reports. However, Himmler tended to distrust them, and described Ohlendorf as 'an unsoldierly type, and a damned intellectual'. Another perhaps more trusted intellectual was Dr Werner Best, for some while an assistant to Heydrich and later to take charge of Denmark for the regime, and SS-Colonel Dr Franz Six, dean of a faculty in the University of Berlin, who was to be ear-marked to take charge in Great Britain once the anticipated invasion had taken place.

Typical of the other wing of the SS – the ill-educated, insensitive, thug-like men who dealt out barbaric treatment in the camps and prisons – was Rudolf Hoess himself, who, as we have seen, was trained by Eicke at Dachau. Hoess, like many barbarians, was a sentimentalist, spilling out his ill-judged pity largely upon himself. His memoirs offer us a unique human document, the revelations of a man with just enough intelligence to describe himself in some detail, but utterly lacking in any sense of due proportion or moral self-appraisal commensurate with the enormity of the crime he undertook for the regime at Auschwitz. For him genocide became a career, elevating him to a rank and a degree of trust in the SS which he could never have approached in any other service. The SS stood in particular need at the lower end of its spectrum of such loyal men as Hoess, the faithful thugs who took

SS support unit in position on the Czech border September, 1938

no special pleasure in sadism but who quickly grew impervious to its practice by the men and women at their command. Many of their victims were their social and intellectual superiors, against whom they bore a jealous grudge. Newcomers to the concentration camps often thought that the anxious revelation of their high social, professional, and intellectual status might gain them some modest privilege in captivity. It only brought them added blows from the barbarians, and an immediate assignment to the filthiest jobs that could be found. In the eyes of the thug, the only good intellectual was a degraded one.

To find the men it wanted to carry out the dirtier work, the SS recruited from the prisons, whether warders or criminals themselves seemed to make but little difference. In fact, it would seem that there was some difficulty before the war in keeping the full time ranks of the SS filled with suitable recruits on what remained until the war years, a voluntary basis. Hoess had in fact taken part in a particularly brutal murder in 1923, and had received a ten year sentence. He had been released, however, in 1928, and had first met Himmler while he was working in a 'folk' agricultural centre. His progress in the SS was noticeably speedy. He was a guard at Dachau in 1934. In 1935 he became a block-leader, in 1936 an SS sergeant-major. In the same year he was commissioned an SS second-lieutenant. Then in 1939 he became commandant of the newly established camp at Sachsenhausen. After war had begun, he was made commandant of Auschwitz, and he ended with the rank of SS Lieutenant-Colonel.

Behind him lay an inhuman form of religious upbringing. Questioned by Dr G M Gilbert, one of the American prison psychologists during the trial at Nuremberg, where Hoess became one of the principal witnesses, he proved to be full of explanations about himself: 'Yes, I was brought up in a very strict Catholic tradition. My father . . . was very strict and fanatical . . . dedicating me to God and the priesthood . . . I had to pray and go to church endlessly, do penance over the slightest misdeed.'

He constantly lamented his past loneliness; although married, he seemed to have had little feeling for his wife. He was at pains, however, to insist on his 'normality': 'I am entirely normal. Even while I was doing this extermination work, I led a normal family life . . . . Perhaps it was a peculiarity of mine, but I always felt best when alone . . . . That was the thing which disturbed my wife most; I was so self-sufficient. I never had friends or a close relationship with anybody – even in my youth.'

Hoess's whole career turned on obeying orders, which he had neither the inclination nor the intelligence seriously to question: 'We SS men were not supposed to think about these things; it never even occurred to us . . . It was something already taken for granted that the Jews were to blame for everything . . . . We just never heard anything else . . . . Our military and ideological training took for granted that we had to protect Germany from the Jews.'

Once Hoess obtained authority himself, he merely moved up the chain of command, receiving his orders from Himmler and exacting their observance from his men. Once he became a prisoner himself and was ordered to admit what he had done, he stood on the witness stand at Nuremberg and revealed every appalling detail with the same fearful, complacent obedience – the pride of the faithful steward called to make his account. His statements made at Nuremberg will be quoted later.

During the 1930s, when the concentration camps were being considerably increased, their reputations as centres where brutality was practised spread as 'rumour' among the German people. Many political prisoners were at this stage released after a term of remedial 'treatment'; they were enjoined to say nothing about what went on inside, on pain of being hauled back for further 'rehabilitation'. But their very silence, when indeed they observed it, enhanced the rumours, while those who talked, however guardedly, only helped to make these centres of detention a much-feared form of sanction against those who might dare openly to oppose the rule of Hitler.

As the years passed, the camps increased in number: among the leading centres were Sachsenhausen (near Berlin-Oranienburg) in 1936, Buchenwald (near Weimar) in 1937, Flossenbürg (in the Upper Palatinate) and Mauthausen (near Linz, Hitler's birthplace in Austria) in 1938, and Ravensbrück (near Fürstenburg in Mecklenburg), the camp for women, in May 1939. These camps, and others, overflowed into various subsidiaries, minor centres of detention attached to the parent camps as their headquarters.

The rapid increase in the number of camps followed on events which represented the expansion of the regime's war against society – the Austrian *Anschluss* of March 1938, the virulent pogrom against the Jews throughout Germany in November of the same year, the two successive advances against Czechoslovakia, the first incorporating the Sudetenland into Germany after the Munich agreement in September 1938, and the second when Hitler invaded Bohemia and Moravia in March 1939. If Himmler's statistics are to be trusted, only 8,000 prisoners were being 'treated' early in January 1937. According to statistics given in *The Anatomy of the SS State*, prisoners amounted to 10,000 late in 1937, while the successive waves of arrests following the events of 1937–39 brought the estimated population of the greatly enlarged number of camps to some 25,000 by the outbreak of the war.

Prisoners were not allowed to sit around while undergoing their remedial ideological 'treatment'. They were soon converted into labour forces occupied, for example, in land reclamation or the enlargement of existing camps and the construction of entirely new ones. It did not take Himmler's workmanlike mind long to grasp that the growing labour forces at his disposal in the camps could be turned to profit on behalf of the SS, so that the movement might increasingly pay for itself instead of drawing on state funds. It might even, with some foresight, acquire considerable capital wealth. Companies were registered, *Deutsche Ausrüstungswerke* (for armaments) and *Deutsche Erd-und Steinwerke* (quarries) to exploit the prison labour, in effect

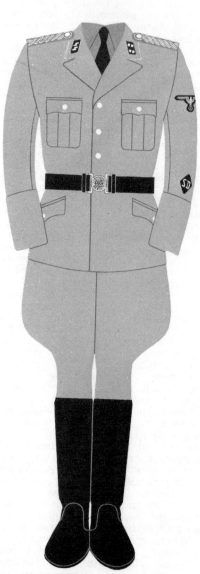

SS UNIFORMS
Major of the Sicherheitsdienst (SD)
– the security service

Sergeant of the Allegemeine-SS (main body)

Sturmabteilungen (SA) – the storm trooper

Allegemeine-SS man: uniform and dagger

Himmler's uniform as Reichsführer-SS

Top left: Luger P.08, used by uniformed Gestapo and SS. *Top right:* Walther PPK, favoured by plain-clothes Gestapo. *Above:* Erma, police sub-machine gun

slave-labour, in quarrying stone, producing gravel, and manufacturing bricks and cement. As early as 1934, a tough working-class ex-naval officer, Oswald Pohl, had been put in charge of what might be called the business management section of the SS administration. A distinct rivalry was in fact to develop between that section of the SS, headed by Heydrich, which looked on the camps as centres of punishment and, later, of liquidation, and this other section, headed by Pohl, which aimed at developing the principle of slave-labour in order to make money. Himmler, following the basic policy of Hitler, which was to divide and rule, backed both policies at once. Authority within the SS for the control and administration of the camps, grew complex during the pre-war years of expansion.

Neither Wilhelm Frick, the Minister of the Interior, nor Franz Gürtner, the Minister of Justice, could call the SS or the Gestapo to account. Both tried in vain to establish powers to prevent the SS and Gestapo from seizing citizens and keeping them in 'protective custody' without trial.

As we have seen, in 1936 Hitler announced that any decision proclaimed by Himmler, acknowledged now the Chief of German Police, should carry the same legal weight as ministerial decrees. In a Prussian state law of February 1936, the duties of the Gestapo were redefined as follows: 'The duty of the Gestapo is to investigate and suppress all anti-State tendencies throughout Prussia, to assemble and evaluate the results of any unrest . . . Neither the instructions nor the affairs of the Gestapo will be open to review by the administrative courts.'

Though the Gestapo was supposed to work in collaboration with the Ministry of the Interior, any proper reference of its activities to the minister or his officials was disregarded by Heydrich and his agents.

Dr Werner Best, Heydrich's deputy in the Secret State Police Office at this time, wrote as follows after the enactment of this new law in Germany's premier state: 'With the establishment of the National Socialist Führer State, Germany for the first time has a system of government

53

which derives from a living idea its legitimate right to resist, with all the coercive means at the disposal of the State, any attack on the present form of the State and its leadership . . . Any attempt to gain recognition for or even to uphold different political ideas will be ruthlessly dealt with, as a symptom of illness which threatens the healthy unity of the indivisible national organism . . . To discover the enemies of the State, to watch them and to render them harmless at the right moment is the preventive police duty of a political police. In order to fulfil this duty the political police must be free to use every means suited to achieve the required end . . . It is no more possible to lay down legal norms for the means to be used by a political police than it is possible to anticipate for all time to come every form of subversive attack or every other threat to the State . . . . From these inescapable facts there has developed the concept of the political police as a new and unique body for the protection of the State whose members, in addition to their official duties, regard themselves as belonging to a fighting formation.'

Thus by 1936 the SS and the Gestapo could be regarded as immune from all formal interference by the State under the former Constitution, while from the point of view of the German public two areas of legal sanction operated side by side – State justice as defined by the Constitution, and the rule of 'law' imposed by Hitler. This rule by Hitler has been described as an 'extra-constitutional Führer-authority', an authority which invariably took precedence when any divergence arose concerning civil rights. Hitler's dictatorship was based on government by 'emergency' decree, both written and unwritten, and Germany was held by Hitler to be in a state of continuous emergency from 1933 to 1945.

With the teeth of the SA drawn after the Röhm purge, Himmler's SS forces became the official 'arm' of the regime, with virtually complete control over the civilian life of the country. Only the men in the standing armed forces themselves were technically free from interference by the SS and the Gestapo – the Gestapo, for example, were

unable to arrest an army officer. If they had evidence against him, all they could do was pass their information to Army Intelligence, the growing department headed from 1935 by Admiral Canaris, a secret opponent of the regime, and a man prepared to allow his section to become from 1938 a centre for active resistance to Hitler. Further extraordinary intrigue sprang from this unique situation. Within the two rival services – the official armed forces directly responsible to Hitler, as Führer and Supreme Commander, and the SS and secret police established under Himmler – there were two rival intelligence services, that controlled by Heydrich for the SS (the SD) and the *Abwehr* (Army Intelligence), controlled by Canaris. Canaris was seventeen years older than Heydrich, and had once been his superior officer in the navy. Now they were on wary, watchful social terms, enacting the part of colleagues. Heydrich played croquet from time to time with Canaris, and the violin with the Admiral's wife, since she delighted in chamber music.

Meanwhile the SS grew in numbers, taking into account its great part-time 'reserve'. Speaking in January 1937 to an assembly of army officers, Himmler revealed that his concentration camp guards, the Death's Head Unit, stood at 3,500 men, and that in addition to the SS, which numbered 20,000, the German uniformed police stood at 90,000. In *The Anatomy of the SS State*, the breakdown of the strength of the SS immediately pre-war is given as follows: armed SS units, including the Death's Head guards, some 25,000; the *Allgemeine* SS, the general body of the SS, some 200,000. There were in 1937 three special SS commando units in existence who were later, in wartime, to become the initial formations in the *Waffen* or Field SS – these were organized with special future wartime duties in mind, and were called the *Leibstandarte Adolf Hitler*, *Standarten Germania*, and *Deutschland*. Certain ex-army officers and other disciplinarians formed the hard core of commanders put in charge of these fighting units – Sepp Dietrich, a former chauffeur, now an SS Major-General, and SS General von dem Bach-Zelewski.

Sepp Dietrich

Paul Haaser, a former Lieutenant-General in the German army, was entrusted with the task of instructing these SS units when, in 1935, Hitler ordered them to receive a full military training of the highest standard. Between 1935 and 1939 these para-military units increased their strength from some 9,000 to some 18,000 men. They were not regarded as police, though their status remained strictly SS. They were soldiers recruited and trained to preserve the stability of the civilian population in time of war. Hitler regarded them as special formations at his own disposal rather than at Himmler's. No risks were being taken.

From 1936, Himmler was prepared to go on record by making both public and closed speeches about his ideals for the SS. In July 1936 he spoke at a ceremony to commemorate the thousandth anniversary of the death of Heinrich I, founder of the German state. 'Henry the Fowler,' cried Himmler, 'never forgot that the strength of the German people lies in the purity of their blood.' The following year, in January 1937,

Himmler delivers his 'Henry the Fowler' speech in 1936

as we have seen, the *Reichsführer SS* was invited to address a closed group of army officers assembled for political indoctrination in view of the war which lay ahead. His speech gives us a first-hand account of the origin and conception of the SS, and of the principles for which Himmler wanted it to stand. He showed how its 'noble ideal' sprang from the original duty of its members when the SS had enjoyed the special responsibility of protecting the speakers whose words had initiated Party doctrine a decade and more ago. Then he rode his favourite hobby horse, the importance of protecting good Germanic blood and increasing the sound Nordic stock in Europe. At first, he said, the SS men had received no money; it had even been necessary for each man to provide his own uniform. Now, in 1937, even though only one in ten of those asking to join was accepted, the ranks of the SS stood at no less than 210,000. 'In the case of every recruit,' he said, 'we ask for the political reputation of his parents, brothers and sisters, the record of his ancestry as far back as 1750.' He

57

described the 'keep-fit' routine for all SS men (including no less than himself) between eighteen (the earliest recruiting age) and fifty, and the maintenance of their mental health by studying *Mein Kampf* during weekly periods of instruction. Then he dealt with the various specialist sections of the SS – the SD, 'the great ideological Intelligence service of the Party, and, in the long run, of the State', and the Death's Head Units whose fearful, purifying task it was to control the 'offal of criminals and freaks' in the concentration camps. 'Hardly another nation would be as humane as we are,' he added.

Finally, he spoke with pride of his Reich police: 'It is the obligation of the SS and the police to solve positively the problem of internal security.' All this, he concluded, was to serve the great cause of German racial superiority: 'We are more valuable than the others who do now, and always will, surpass us in numbers. We are more valuable because our blood enables us to invent more than others, to lead our people better than others. Let us clearly realize, the next decades signify a struggle leading to the extermination of the subhuman opponents in the whole world who fight Germany, the basic people of the Northern race, bearer of the culture of mankind.'

This pursuit of race led to some strange results. In 1936 the first SS maternity homes were founded. They were to be Himmler's special pride, and all SS men, and especially those who perversely chose to remain bachelors, had deductions made from their pay in order to support these centres where pure-blooded babies, both legitimate and illegitimate, could be born. The *Lebensborn* (Fount of Life) homes, as they were called, provided both mother and child with a comfortable, and suitably endoctrinated environment. Himmler told his men to be fruitful and multiply through the right female stock; his famous decree of 1939 exhorted every

Anti-Semitism before the war. *Below:* SA men impose a boycott on a Jewish department store in 1933. *Right:* Jews forced to wear the Star of David

man to father a child before he went to battle. The SS birthrate, however, was scarcely encouraging; in August 1936 the average size of SS families stood at only between one and two children each. There was an obvious need to supplement this shortfall by encouraging illegimate breeding, but it is quite incorrect to assume, as certain sensationalist post-war writers have done, that the *Lebensborn* homes were in effect places where desirable SS men were put out to stud. A much more sinister method of supplementing the population came in time of war through the confiscation of children of suitable stock in the occupied countries and rearing them in German foster homes.

The notorious Nuremberg Race Laws of 1935 stemmed directly from the Nazi conception of 'Aryan' superiority. At one time or another most of the countries of Europe have used their Jewish minorities as scapegoats and initiated pogroms, confiscations, evictions, and enforced migrations. Certain aspects of reactionary German thought in the 19th century, as we have seen, were permeated with anti-Semitism, and Vienna, in particular, became a centre for anti-Jewish feeling. The Nazis, therefore, had chosen the Jews as well as the Communists as their scapegoats, usually identifying the two in a single cloud of opprobrium.

Open persecution of the Jews began with the establishment of the regime, and culminated in the pre-war years with the nation-wide pogrom of 9th November 1938, the so-called *Reichskristallnacht* (the Night of Broken Glass, an ironic title). The Jews had soon learned from 1933 that they were to be regarded as social pariahs; they were excluded from the professions, from the civil service, from the army, from public practice in the arts or sport. Jewish businesses were boycotted, and in every public place notices were put up warning all Jews to keep away – they could not bathe with racial Germans, or sit in the public parks. Many trades were forbidden them. The aim was to freeze them out of German society.

By 1939 Germany's 600,000 Jews had been reduced to some 210,000. Some had already died through the

persecution, but the majority had fled the country; no less than 50,000 left in 1933, and Great Britain alone received, either permanently or in transit, some 60,000 German Jews during the years 1936–37. The great tragedy of German Jewry was enhanced by the very restricted legal entry into Palestine decreed by the British, who held the mandate, as a result of Arab pressure – 15,000 only were permitted legal entry during 1939, the year following the November pogrom.

German policy at this stage was to rid herself of her Jews at the expense of any nation willing to adopt them: their property was confiscated by the State, and for the most part they emerged as penniless refugees. The SS and the Gestapo used their 'influence' to hasten the lucrative emigration of people Hitler no longer wanted. The Gestapo became the central authority which, at a price, gave exit permits to anxious and fearful Jews. An extraordinary situation arose when members of the Zionist underground formed to sponsor and organize illegal immigration into Palestine found themselves working in association with the SS and Gestapo officers in Germany and Austria for the express purpose of making the countries 'Jew-free'. A common policy united these deadliest of enemies. SS Captain Adolf Eichmann readily agreed to establish a training camp for young Jews in Austria where they could learn farming in anticipation of being smuggled illegally into Palestine.

For Himmler, anti-Semitism had become an obsession from his early youth, whereas with Goebbels it was an acquired characteristic and with Göring, a kind of dirty joke. In the end, it was left to Himmler, with the help of his aide, Heydrich, to rid the Reich of Jews. The anti-Jewish policy which phased its way through Himmler's tidy mind found its first expression in the encouragement of mass emigration, next in mass-eviction and expulsion to the east, and lastly, after 1940, in the 'final solution' of slave-labour combined with genocide. He recognized from the start that the Jewish question needed the most careful study, and to this end he had appointed the unemployed commercial traveller, Adolf Eichmann, to act as his Jewish 'specialist'. Eichmann, born a German, had been reared in Linz in Austria by a domineering step-mother. He had been a frail child, a Protestant in a Catholic environment, unhappy at his school and therefore ill-educated, and in young manhood frequently out of work. When at last he had found his haven in the SS he became a corporal in the SD under Heydrich, and set about acquiring a spurious 'expertise' in Jewish affairs. He even started to learn Hebrew, and paid a brief visit to Palestine. This had been round 1934, when he was twenty-eight.

By 1938 he was an SS Captain in charge of the office for Jewish emigration in Austria – but, as he hastened to point out when interrogated long after the war, he was 'no anti-Semite'. 'I was,' he said, 'just politically opposed to Jews because they were stealing the breath of life from us.' Ironically, he called himself a Zionist who wanted the Jews to have 'a firm soil under their feet'. 'I was a fervent nationalist,' he said on the stand at Jerusalem, 'I regarded the Jews as opponents, but not as opponents who must be exterminated.' Under his aegis, 100,000 Jews left Austria between the annexation in March 1938 and the beginning of the war, a period of eighteen months.

The Austrian *Anschluss*, in fact, had shown how well-organized the SS had become. Clad in a new field-grey uniform, and accompanied by his specialist staff, Himmler had flown to Vienna overnight to seize at the earliest possible moment any useful document upon which he and his assistants could lay their hands, and so acquire evidence against every known enemy of the new regime. Austria had fallen in a matter of hours, and the local SS provided Himmler with a number of recruits whom he regarded as invaluable, including Ernst Kaltenbrunner, head of the SS in Austria. Everyone of any present or future importance in the German SS seemed now to be in Vienna – Himmler, Heydrich, Schellenberg, and Eichmann. Kaltenbrunner, a lawyer with an all-but expres-

Ernst Kaltenbrunner

Adolf Eichmann

sionless face and huge, clumsy hands was in less than five years to succeed Heydrich as head of the Reich Security Office. On the arrival of Hitler and Himmler in Austria, thousands committed suicide, and the signal for the mass-emigration of Austrian Jews was given. Within a matter of weeks, 79,000 arrests were made, as Arthur Seyss-Inquart, the new Nazi Chancellor of Austria, admitted when on trial after the war at Nuremberg, where he sat in the dock alongside Kaltenbrunner.

Mass-emigration, therefore, represented Nazi policy for the Jews throughout the pre-war period. At this stage, with the Jews streaming out of Germany and Austria leaving their wealth behind them, there could scarcely be said to be a Jewish 'problem' for the Nazis. The great concentration of European Jews, and these mostly impoverished, lay to the east outside these Germanic territories – 3,300,000 in Poland, 2,100,000 in western Russia, and a further million and a half in Czechoslovakia, Hungary, and Rumania. By September 1939 only some 280,000 Jews were left in Germany and Austria. Planned genocide of the Jews by the SS did not begin until the occupation of Poland and western Russia faced the Nazi leaders with a sudden acquired control of some six million Jews, ten times as many as there had

ever been in Germany, and twenty times as many as there were left in 1939. Since the Slavs, too, constituted yet another inferior race in Nazi eyes, mass destruction was to seem the only 'final solution' to this tragic racial 'problem'.

Hitler was to make it the special privilege of the SS to resolve it.

In the preparation for war, Himmler sought to have his place. The military ambitions of his youth were never wholly set aside, and for a while, as at the very end of the war, Hitler finally gave way and allowed him to exercise a wholly disastrous, not to say ludicrous, period of command on both the eastern and western fronts. In 1938, however, the tension between Himmler and the High Command of the Armed Forces (OKW) found its expression in the underhand devices by means of which Field-Marshal Werner von Blomberg, the Minister of Defence, and Colonel-General Baron Werner von Fritsch, the Commander-in-Chief, were 'removed' to suit Hitler's convenience. The former fell from grace by contracting a marriage with a former prostitute whose police record did not mature until after the ceremony, which had been witnessed by both Hitler and Göring. The Gestapo was even more directly implicated in the fall of Fritsch, against whom a completely false charge of homosexuality was prepared on the

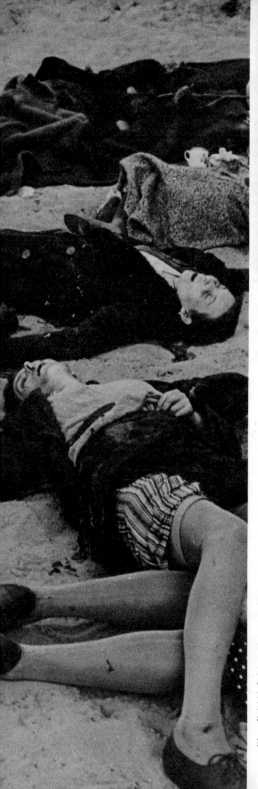

Nazi brutality at its most cynical. Fake Polish atrocities

strength of the testimony of a single, corrupt witness. OKW was so affronted by these disgraceful machinations that they managed to force Hitler to permit the formation of a court of honour to examine this unbelievable testimony. Göring presided, and had not the dramatic events of the Austrian *Anschluss* interrupted the hearings, the army might well have succeeded in exposing the Gestapo's technique of procuring evidence, and so disgracing both Himmler and Heydrich. As it was, Göring cut short the hearing and, whilst declaring Fritsch's name to be cleared, saved the Gestapo from exposure. It had all been due, he said, to an unhappy misunderstanding. Fritsch, utterly disillusioned, retired into obscurity, and committed virtual suicide while serving in the line during the invasion of Poland the following year, when he allowed himself to be killed.

Himmler, however, was fully prepared to act should war break out.

Evidence was produced at Nuremberg that secret SS units, forerunners of the murderous Action Groups which were to conduct mass extermination in Poland and in Russia, were poised ready in 1938 to follow the German army into Czechoslovakia, following in the wake of the invading forces, 'cleaning-up' and 'liquidating' all civilian opposition as they went and annihilating Jews and Communists. These initial Action Groups were not, in the outcome, needed at this present stage. As a result of the Munich agreement, the Sudetenland passed 'peacefully' into German hands, as did the occupation of Bohemia and Moravia the following year and the creation of a protectorate in Slovakia. In the Sudetenland itself, Himmler had planned to take command of the German Henlein's local Free Corps in the event of trouble. The attempt was to prove abortive, and the Free Corps were rendered harmless. A Free Corps leader, however, Karl Hermann Frank, became Himmler's local SS and police chief, controlling security on the *Reichsführer SS's* behalf.

Himmler was permitted to undertake a single, inglorious exploit at the start of the war with Poland. This was the so-called 'Operation Gleiwitz'. A fake border incident, planned by the Gestapo chief, Heinrich Müller, was put in the hands of an unscrupulous adventurer, Alfred Naujocks, who was later to desert to the Americans in 1944. With the aid of some Polish uniforms and a few prisoners obtained from the camps, Poland was made to appear to have started the war on Germany by attacking the radio station at Gleiwitz. The dead and the dying, dressed in the appropriate uniforms, lay there for photographs to be taken by army and press photographers. The prisoners from the camps were brought in for sacrifice under a code phrase, 'canned goods'; they were given fatal injections by an SS doctor, and then 'wounded' by gunshot. Such was one of the border 'incidents' used to justify Hitler's merciless *Blitzkrieg* upon Poland, a campaign which was to last a bare three weeks.

Wartime role of the SS

Poland, to a far greater extent than either Austria or even the 'protectorates' of Czechoslovakia, became a test case for the thoroughness of Nazi occupation and the sudden imposition of an alien police state. The Poles were a proud, not to say a militant people, who tried in vain to pit their old-fashioned, chivalric methods of defence against the modernity of Hitler's mechanized armies with their bombers in the skies and tanks on the ground. The Nazi Panzer divisions rolled their way in; they proved all but unopposable, except for the final, hardcore defence of Warsaw. The collapse of Poland militarily did not mean the collapse of Polish resistance, but this long-suffering territory, whose boundaries had been subject to dispute for centuries, found itself once more in the hands of a cruel conqueror. Or rather, two conquerors; for, by the secret clauses in their non-aggression pact of August 1939, the two great ideological opponents, Nazi Germany and Soviet Russia, had concurred over the division of Poland in advance of Hitler's invasion. The eastern territories were occupied by the Russians, the western territories incorporated into Germany, while the ill-fated rump in the middle was called the Government-General and put in the charge of one of the Nazi intellectuals, Dr Hans Frank, a lawyer aged thirty-nine who had acted since 1933 as one of Hitler's principal legal authorities.

Poland became the first full-scale operation conducted by the SS in wartime. To them and not to the army fell the task of reorientating and 'cleansing' the country. It was only to be expected that Poland's frontiers would be radically adjusted by Hitler so that former German territories would return to the Reich, and the isolated area of East Prussia would be geographically re-united within greater Germany. Frank's Government-General, with its headquarters in Cracow, included Warsaw in its area, and represented in all about one quarter of the Polish territory before the invasion, and one-third its population. Frank therefore ruled the

Hans Frank, Reichsprotektor of the Government-General of Poland

lives of some twelve million people.

Frank took up his new appointment as Poland's civil governor in October 1939, following a hasty, ten-minute interview with Hitler, during which he learned of his new responsibilities. His forty-two-volume diary, recording the events of his open tyranny with a near-hysteric megalomania, was used in evidence against him on the stand at Nuremberg, where his unstable personality led him to adopt the postures of a penitent.

Faced at Nuremberg with the incontrovertible facts of the war crimes which took place inside his territory (the extermination camps of Treblinka, Belzec, and Lublin-Maidanek were in the Government-General, though Auschwitz was outside it), Frank fell back on what was to become the final excuse of almost all top Nazis when they were cornered after the war – that he had known

nothing about what Himmler and the SS did. They were, he claimed, a law unto themselves, and refused to divulge what took place in any area they appropriated. 'I was never in Maidanek, Treblinka, or Auschwitz,' declared Frank at Nuremberg. Nevertheless, in his diary, he makes it very clear that he was in full sympathy with what the SS were actually doing. For example, he records his own words spoken at a 'Cabinet' meeting in December 1941: 'As far as the Jews are concerned, I want to tell

you quite frankly that they must be done away with in one way or another . . . I know that many of the measures carried out against the Jews in the Reich at present are being criticized . . . Before I continue, I want to beg you to agree with me on the following formula: We will on principle have pity on the German people only and nobody else in the whole world. The others, too, had no pity on us. As an old National-Socialist I must say this: This would only be a partial success if the whole of

Jewry survive it, while we had shed our best blood in order to save Europe. My attitude towards the Jews will, therefore, be based only on the expectation that they must disappear. They must be done away with. . . . Gentlemen, I must ask you to rid yourselves of all feeling of pity. We must annihilate the Jews, wherever we find them and wherever it is possible, in order to maintain the structure of the Reich as a whole.'

The prime task of the SS in wartime was to rid the growing empire acquired by the *Herrenvolk* of every person who threatened their development – first of all, opponents in their midst, rebel Germans and resistance workers; second, men and women of the Resistance in the occupied countries, whether of the political Right or Left; third, all unwanted peoples, more especially Jews, Gypsies and Slavs. When the war with Russia began in 1941, all known Communist officials and representatives had likewise to be destroyed as automatic partisans. The burden of these tasks fell on Himmler and on Heydrich.

The actual secret orders or 'arrangements' for genocide have been traced back to 1941, by which year it had become what might be called a masterplan with Heydrich in charge of the administrative details. Nazi policy was always ad hoc and opportunist; that is, the Nazi leaders did what they chose to do as and when the necessity arose – though behind it all, as a guiding instinct, lay Hitler's imperial dream as outlined in *Mein Kampf*. So long as there were rich

Left above and below: **Polish prisoners of war.** *Above:* **Jewish workers are herded across a Warsaw street**

Jews to pillage and a channel for mass emigration, the Nazis were obviously happy to enjoy the proceeds and 'arrange' for the Jews to leave. When war came and closed these channels, or most of them, as well as vastly increasing the number of Jews and unwanted aliens who fell into German hands, other devices for riddance had to be adopted. Punitive assassination had to be stepped up, and this was obviously not a task for the army (which in many sectors was still respectable enough to be horrified at such things, though some men played the 'voyeur' with their cameras), but for the specially trained, specially toughened assassins in Himmler's Action Groups who did the actual work as a matter of cold duty to the State. Long before the secret orders which activated the genocide camps of 1941–45 came into force, punitive assassination in the worst pockets of resistance was put into action by the SS in the name of the Reich's security.

To understand when and where this could be done, we must understand how the Nazis graded and governed their occupied territories. Hitler's concept of conquest was quite clearly outlined in *Mein Kampf* and had been available for all to read throughout the later 1920s and the 1930s. The first principle of German expansion to the east was to secure *lebensraum*, living space, for every

69

Dr Werner Best

pure blooded German. Remember the words of Hitler: 'Never consider the Reich secure unless, for centuries to come, it is in a position to give every descendant of our race a piece of ground and soil that he can call his own. Never forget that the most sacred of all rights in this world is man's right to the earth which he wishes to cultivate for himself and that the holiest of all sacrifices is that of the blood poured out for it.'

Hitler held himself to be the third great unifier of the German people, following in the wake of Charlemagne and Bismarck. Hence he called his regime the Third Reich. The first phase of his empire Hitler acquired by sheer horse trading with old-fashioned diplomats who despised him until they found he had out-witted them and got what he wanted without resort to warfare. When he was ready to fight, he fought his old-fashioned opponents by modern methods, the *Blitzkrieg*, and so added two-thirds of Poland to his empire by right of actual conquest. Now two wholly alien territories were in his power – Czechoslovakia and Poland.

For administrative purposes, ter-ritory absorbed into the Reich was governed, like Nazi Germany, by being divided into *Gaue,* or Districts, controlled by the Party Gauleiters. In Poland, these Germanized areas were cleared of unwanted, non-

German people and 're-stocked' with German families uprooted from their homes further east. The non-incor-porated territories became 'protec-torates' under control of three joint authorities – a civilian Governor-General (such as Frank in central Poland, the Government-General), the commander of the German occupa-tion forces, and the commanding officer of the SS and Security Police (the Gestapo). When the Nazis moved north and west and acquired coun-tries the importance of which was primarily strategic, the supreme con-troller was normally an army com-mandant. But, as the countries such as Norway, France, and Belgium were to know to their cost, the real watchdogs over civilian behaviour remained the local SS and Gestapo.

Hitler called his European empire the 'New Order' in Europe, and the status of the countries he occupied differed from territory to territory. The 'protectorates', such as Bohemia-Moravia and Slovakia, were puppet-states under direct German control. Other areas were left nominally freer, with puppet governments of their own – like the Quisling government in Norway or the Vichy government in central and southern France. Some, like Belgium, retained their normal administration, operating under overall German control. In countries such as Denmark, which Hitler held to be racially akin to Germany and where he hoped the people would come to regard Ger-many as an ally, the administration imposed was relatively light – in fact, Dr Werner Best of the SS was to prove one of the more 'reasonable' of the Nazi overlords, very different from Frank in Poland and Rosenberg in the occupied areas of the Soviet Union. All these territories, however, were, with varying degrees of severity, police states.

Once in occupation, Hitler totally disregarded the terms of the Hague Convention designed to protect the interests of subject peoples in war-time. Technically, Germany as a signatory of the Convention, should have observed those clauses dealing with the rights of conquered peoples. Hitler should have retained the laws governing the civil rights of citizens in each occupied country, respected their property (which, if requisitioned, should still have remained the property of the owner), and retained the established taxation system, using taxation only to cover the costs of administration and occupation of the country itself. To do otherwise was not only to rob the individual and the State, but to deprive the local citizens of their basic civil rights.

For Hitler, boundaries meant nothing if he saw advantage in changing them. Austria, the Sudeten territory, and western Poland were not the only territories directly incorporated into the new, greater Germany. Others that followed were the Belgian areas of Eupen, Malmédy, and Moresnet (July 1940) as well as Danzig and Memel, all of them formerly incorporated in Germany before 1918. Other incorporated territories were Alsace-Lorraine and Luxembourg. The announcement of these changes immediately put the citizenship status of the inhabitants in doubt. Families of German stock were given full German citizenship after due investigation. Other 'loyalist' citizens, who were unfortunate enough not to be German, were granted a form of second-class German citizenship; they became, in effect, associate citizens *(Staatsangehörige)*. But the rest in these incorporated territories lost all their former rights; the best way out for them was to remove themselves into the areas of their country which had not been incorporated. Jews, of course, became stateless overnight, like the refugees who had fled Germany before the war.

The winter of 1939–40 was exceptionally hard. Himmler issued an order, dated 9th October, which decreed that some half million Jews and inferior-grade Slavs had to be forcibly moved from the German-incorporated area of Poland to make room for about half this number of families of German origin who had suddenly found themselves in the Russian sector of Poland, or in the Baltic states annexed by Russia. This had been foreseen as part of the secret agreement between Soviet Russia and Nazi Germany the previous summer. The appalling task of effecting

Odilo Globoznik

this interchange in mid-winter was most ineffectually supervised by Walter Darré, Himmler's earnest friend who had taught him such uncompromising racialism. Darré's administration was constantly thwarted by the various overlapping functions of Frank in the Government-General, and those of the SS commanders in the areas involved – Friedrich Krueger, an expert in street-fighting, and the Austrian, Odilo Globocnik, an alcoholic, whom even Himmler had eventually to displace for criminal exploitation and theft. Darré was no match for these unscrupulous men who were enjoying their first taste of absolute authority over the fate of large numbers of human beings.

The immediate task of the SS was to shift the Polish Jews into ghettoes within the Government-General. Their vacated properties were taken over temporarily by a trustee agency responsible for administering the re-settlement. 'Our task,' said Himmler, 'is to Germanize the east, not in the old sense of bringing the German language and laws to people living in that area, but to ensure that in the east only people of genuinely German, Teutonic blood shall live.' Heydrich's orders of 21st September to the SS Action Groups were specific: '1. Jews to be moved to the towns as quickly as possible; 2. Jews to be moved out of the Reich into Poland; 3. The re-

The entrance to the Warsaw ghetto

maining 30,000 Gypsies also to be moved into Poland; 4. Jews in the German territories (that is to say those previously held by Poland) to be systematically deported by goods train.'

The scale of this movement was very great. After some delays, it began in December 1939. 250,000 Poles and people of German stock from the Baltic states were to be sent to western Poland (now part of the Reich) all from the Russian-held territories. Half a million Jews from western Poland were to be moved into the Government-General, making some two million Jews in all in German-held Poland, the remainder, some 1,300,000 being still in Russian hands. Their turn was to come later. This sudden accumulation of unwanted people during the winter of 1939–40

was what really led to the deliberate adoption of genocide as future Nazi policy.

Almost half a million Jews were walled up in the great ghetto of Warsaw, while the rest were rapidly segregated in other ghettoes and camps improvised during the winter. No Jew was permitted a normal work permit, though his labour could be hired for approved purposes. Confined in these cruel circumstances,

deprived even of meagre rations allowed non-Jewish Poles, the weaker soon began to die without the intervention of genocide. Raul Hilberg, the leading authority on Nazi genocide of the Jews, claims more than half a million died in this way throughout Poland. In the Warsaw ghetto alone, 44,630 died during 1941, while during 1942, a year before the heroic campaign of armed resistance organized in the ghetto, 5,000 were dying on average each month. In October of that year some 60,000 Jews were living in the 300,000 square yards to which the ghetto had by that time been contracted; by then the ghetto was being drained of its non-worker inhabitants in the process of active genocide, while the more corrupt SS men were selling Jewish labour to equally corrupt businessmen by means of black-market deals which side-stepped the armaments works where the remaining Jews were supposed to provide slave-labour. In the ghetto of Lodz, some 30,000 of the original 100,000 inhabitants died between May 1940 and June 1942.

It would appear that in Poland the SS set the pattern for their part in German invasion procedure, and used their most reliable assistants and collaborators to carry out the initial, worst phases of the task. The business of resettlement appears to have been undertaken by a combination of SS shock-troops from the Death's Head Division – numbering some 7,400 – supplemented by Heydrich's Action Groups and by professional German police recruited into the SS.

Heydrich himself dictated a memorandum in July 1940 describing the activities of his Action Groups and the difficulties they met with – in certain cases through the resistance put up by German army commanders, difficulties he did not want to see repeated during the invasion of the Soviet Union: 'In all previous cases – Austria, the Sudetenland, Bohemia and Moravia – police Action Groups went in with the advancing troops in accordance with a special order from the Führer; in Poland they went in with the fighting troops. As a result of their preparatory work they were able through arrests, confiscations and safeguarding of important political material, systematically to deal heavy blows to those world movements hostile to the Reich directed by the emigré, freemason, Jewish and politically hostile ecclesiastical camp. . . .

'Co-operation with the troops below staff level and in many cases with the army staffs was in general good; on the other hand, in many cases the more senior army commanders adopted a fundamentally different approach to the basic suppression of enemies of the State. This approach . . . gave rise to friction and counter orders contravening the political activity undertaken by the Reichsführer SS. . . . The directives governing police activity were exceptionally far-reaching, the liquidation of numerous Polish leading circles running into thousands of persons was ordered; such an order could not be divulged to the general run of military headquarters, still less to members of the staffs; to the uninitiated therefore the action of the police and SS appeared arbitrary, brutal, and unauthorized.'

Himmler was deeply concerned about what had to be done by the SS – but more concerned for those who had to carry out the killings and the evictions than for their victims. In a speech to a closed audience of SS officers made the following year he referred back to the onerous duties performed by these loyal SS men on behalf of all Germans, and why similar tasks must be undertaken so that Europe might be cleansed: 'Exactly the same thing happened in Poland in weather forty degrees below zero, where we had to haul away thousands, tens of thousands, hundreds of thousands, where we had to have the toughness – you should hear this but also forget it again immediately – to shoot thousands of leading Poles, otherwise revenge would have been taken on us later . . . all duties where the proud soldier says: "My God, why do I have to do that, this ridiculous job here!''. It is much easier to go into combat with a company than to suppress an obstructive population of low cultural level, or to carry out executions, or to haul away people, or to evict crying and hysterical women, or to return our German racial brethren across the border from Russia and to take care of them. . . . It is much more difficult . . . . in this silent compulsion work, this silent activity.'

As the Germans moved into a newly occupied territory, therefore, a complex situation arose, which differed considerably according to the 'grade' of occupation you were to live under, and the severity of the rule. There was all the difference between living

in the Government-General of Poland and, for example, Denmark or the British Channel Islands. In Poland, the reign of terror was uppermost, with little distinction between the severity of Frank's civilian administration and the punitive operations of the SS and Gestapo. The nation became a slave state, the interests of whose citizens were completely subordinate to those of their masters. Hitler was quite clear about his intentions in Poland, and made no bones about it. Martin Bormann noted down what he said one evening after dinner in October 1940, in the presence of Frank himself: 'The Poles, in direct contrast to our German workmen, are specially born for hard labour .... There can be no question of improvement for them. On the contrary, it is necessary to keep the standard of life low in Poland, and it must not be permitted to rise. . . . The Government-General should be used by us merely as a source for unskilled labour. . . . It is indispensable to bear

in mind that the Polish landlords must cease to exist; however cruel this may sound, they must be exterminated wherever they are. . . . There should be only one master for the Poles – the Germans. . . . Therefore all representatives of the Polish intelligentsia are to be exterminated. This too sounds cruel, but such is the law of life.

The Poles will also benefit from this, as we look after their health and see to it that they do not starve; but they must never be raised to a higher level, for then they will become anarchists and Communists. It will therefore be proper for the Poles to remain Roman Catholics; Polish priests will receive food from us and will, for that reason, direct their little sheep along the path we favour .... The task of the priest is to keep the Poles quiet, stupid, and dullwitted.'

In Denmark, on the other hand, the 'correct' side of German military and civilian control was uppermost;

Above: A Jewish police force was created inside the Warsaw ghetto.
Below: Jews prepare for removal from the Lodz ghetto (1942)

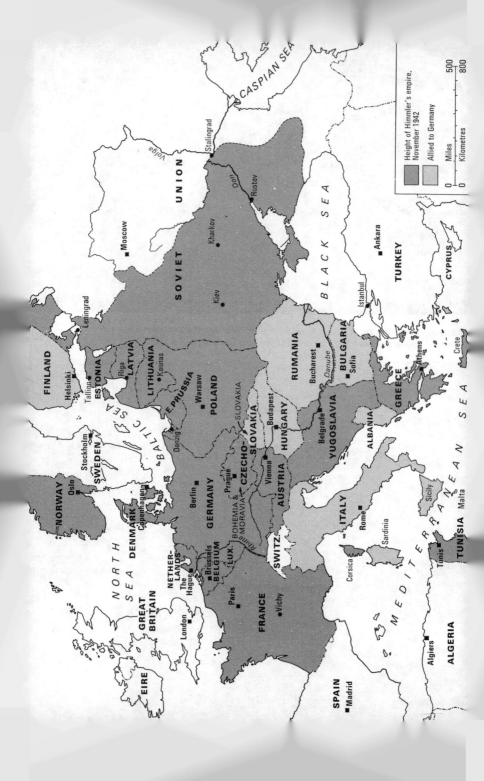

since the Danes were racial kinsmen, they were treated initially as *alliés manqués*, allies, that is, who had unfortunately not been persuaded to throw in their lot with that of their occupiers. They were therefore latent equals. Only resistance, open or underground, was treated with the sudden, stabbing severity characteristic of the cat-and-mouse tactics of the SS and the Gestapo, against whose operations, once launched, there could be no redress. But until August 1943 Denmark remained virtually intact, a democratic monarchy, but under 'protective' custody, though still governing itself according to its normal constitution. As resistance grew, however, German martial law had to be declared. It is well-known that Denmark's small Jewish minority of some 5,000 people received the special protection of King Christian. The Danes were on the whole fortunate in having Dr Werner Best as Reich Plenipotentiary from 1942 to 1945. To save unpleasantness, he connived at the last-minute escape of this minority to Sweden.

One of the more fearful of the powers of the SS and Gestapo in any German-controlled country lay in the notorious decree called *Nacht und Nebel* (literally, Night and Fog, a German cliché for illicit disappearance). This decree of 7th December 1941 was issued as an Army High Command order by Hitler and signed on his behalf by Keitel. This made official policy out of what was already an established practice; anyone could be seized whom the authorities chose to believe endangered German security whatever his nationality and spirited out of the country 'in night and fog' so that no form of local trial or hearing should take place to stir up local feeling. *Nacht und Nebel* applied particularly to France, Holland, and Belgium. The arrest, when made by the Gestapo, would come suddenly, and invariably in the small hours of the morning. The prisoner would be dragged from his house, thrust into some waiting vehicle, and rushed away. Then no amount of entreaty by members of his family, or by others interceding on his behalf, would discover what had happened

to him, or even where he was. He would be tried in Germany, if he were tried at all, and not left to the obscure treatment given to prisoners by the Gestapo. He would, in fact, either be dead, or a nameless number languishing in some Gestapo cell, subject to intermittent interrogation and probably to torture, or condemned to a slow death in a concentration camp. Gross-Rosen and Natzweiler became the camps ear-marked for *Nacht und Nebel* prisoners. No one in authority back in France, or whatever country he came from, would admit to knowing anything about him. Neither the civilian nor the military authority was answerable.

Thus the secret police remained above all open law. For example, in the Netherlands this was expressly stated in a decree issued by the Reich Commissioner on 19th March 1941: 'In fulfilment of his duties the Supreme SS and Police Chief may deviate from existing regulations. . . . . He may promulgate rules and regulations having the force and effect of laws. . . . Such rules and regulations may contain penal provisions subjecting a defendant to fines of unlimited amount and imprisonment.'

The Gestapo, in particular, thrived on such powers. The kind of men who fulfilled this particular service tended to be those who conformed to the right 'image' – whether in uniform or plain clothes, they would enhance their sinister appearance by wearing jackboots and breeches, or black leather overcoats, black gloves and dark glasses. Like Hitler, they knew the importance of such melodrama in the promotion of public terror.

Special courts of law to administer Nazi justice were established in Germany and outside. Here a citizen's case might be arbitrarily 'heard' in order that a directed judgment might be officially served upon him. In the occupied countries, these courts might be either military or civil in origin. The citizen in an occupied country was terrorised just as much by not knowing in advance before what form of 'court' he might be thrust as he was through ignorance of the charge the authorities might confront him with. Punitive fines, confiscation of property, imprisonment,

Dutch Jews on their way to the concentration camp

perhaps all of these, might suddenly come upon him, imposed by men sitting behind tables in military or in SS uniform. The Poles soon learned to their cost what these arbitrary 'courts' meant before the authorities had had time to display posters declaiming what the latest rules and regulations were to be.

Property, land, goods would be confiscated in Poland on the spot. The SS men would arrive; all Jews would be told to assemble in some public place, only to find that their total possessions were to be taken from them. In the west, Jewish property (if not removed and taken to Germany) would be used to reward collaborators, who might suddenly find themselves given, for example, a Jewish shop. Jewish-owned firms would be taken over, and a German, or pro-German management instated. In the same way, the threat of dispossession became a major form of coercion against the better-off sec-

tions of the general population. In any case, any goods of potential value to Germany were subject to confiscation in Poland, and this extended to priceless works of art in both public and private collections. Naturally, gold or holdings in foreign currency or investments disappeared.

Similarly, the currency of an occupied territory could be debased by introducing new rates of exchange in favour of the *Reichsmark*, followed by enforced trading to take advantage of this adjustment. Soldiers, SS men, and German civilians in occupied territory lived handsomely by being able to exchange their inflated certificate money at specially favourable rates against the local currency, and the Reich itself made vast sums when it came to exacting charges for maintaining occupation forces. This situation was made still worse by the system of taxation. In Poland incoming German settlers were exempt from taxes imposed on the Poles themselves. The control of labour was also punitive. Workers were issued with work-books or labour-cards which made them subject to direction or conscription. In the Government-General, this applied to everyone between the ages of eighteen and sixty, and eventually turned the inhabitants into colonial helots working for Germany on minimal wages which were mostly frozen at pre-war level, while the prices of commodities rose with the general inflation. The only further education allowed the Poles was technical training to fit them for their work producing iron, steel, and coal for Germany, while their schools were segregated from those of the better kind set up for children of German racial stock.

In the west, pressure in varying degrees was brought to bear on the younger people to go to Germany as 'voluntary' workers in order to release more men to serve in Germany's fighting services and SS. The voluntary nature of this exile ceased in Belgium, for example, in March 1942, when by decree young people between eighteen and twenty-five could be sent on compulsory war work to Germany. In Denmark, however, such conscription was never introduced, though the national economy was eventually made to suffer in favour of that of Germany. Workers proving difficult, especially in Poland, could be disciplined through withholding their ration books for food or for such services as still existed to help them during sickness or unemployment. At its height, the recruitment of foreign labour reached some five million in Germany. Large numbers came from Poland, but 876,000 were brought in from France.

All these complexities of control merely played into the hands of the SS. All they had to do was discover or frame up some infringement of the regulations and use this as a pretext for their interrogations. The Gestapo on the whole preferred to be neat in such matters, to have at least something on paper against anyone they arrested. They tended to operate behind a screen of dossiers and files, the contents of which they might or might not reveal to their victims.

Over all these manifold tasks Himmler, as *Reichsführer SS*, reigned with Heydrich as his deputy. His principal police forces had been regrouped

in September 1939, after the fall of Poland, under the general title of the Reich Security Office (RSHA, *Reichssicherheitshauptamt*). This had given Himmler's supreme body, the SS, overall control of state police activity, and the elimination of the old distinction between what was a purely Party machine and what ranked as a State machine. All the police services were combined through the creation of RSHA, including the Gestapo.

RSHA was for administrative reasons divided into departments, which included Internal Intelligence (controlling spies and agents inside Germany, with espionage itself grouped, according to interest, in public opinion, racial matters, culture and education, religious interests, industry and labour, upper-class society, and so forth), the Gestapo (with its many branches specialising in watching political subversion at home and in the occupied countries), KRIPO (the criminal police), and External Intelligence (covering not only occupied territories, but all important areas abroad). RSHA headquarters remained at the old address, 8 Prinz Albrecht-Strasse. All RSHA personnel, including uniformed members of the Gestapo, wore SD armbands on their uniforms.

RSHA became a gigantic spider's web which, fortunately on occasion for those caught in its toils, became entangled within itself, and therefore slow and inefficient. Lines became crossed, while internal power-struggles led to stalemates; files became lost, and excessive bureaucracy slowed down action. The Gestapo, which, before the war, had under Heydrich established its network of some twenty-one main centres and thirty-six subsidiary centres, grew during the war to a 1944 figure of 50,000 men, though Kaltenbrunner, who succeeded Heydrich as head of RSHA, admitted to a ceiling of 40,000 only when on trial at Nuremberg after the war. This full-time staff covered Germany and the occupied countries alike, and made additional use of local collaborators and agents everywhere they could be found. Throughout the whole of the war period the Gestapo, as a department of RSHA,

came under Heinrich Müller, 'Gestapo' Müller as he was called. After the war, Müller, a former political police official from Munich, escaped arrest in May 1945 and is now thought to be in Russia, or if not there, in Latin America.

SS recruits could now be directed into the sector for which their talents seemed most appropriate. Promising cadets normally spent three months in each of the three main branches of RSHA before being assigned to any one of them.

As Himmler saw it, RSHA was necessary in order to co-ordinate the manifold political activities which his various forces manipulated in the growing territory of the German empire. He was quite clear about this, and said as much in a detailed order sent out to his heads of departments in June 1942: 'The war has accelerated the political development of the Reich. Particularly in relation to the newly occupied territories, decisions continually have to be taken of decisive importance for the future political development of the Reich itself and therefore in particular for the SS overall. As SS men we shall only be able to enforce the necessary political decisions with adequate energy and pertinacity if those decisions are completely centralized. . . . The necessary adjustment to the prevailing situation can only be ensured if, within the SS, decision upon all political matters rests with one office.

Himmler's ambition to take over forces which operated under other authorities became only too plain in later years. Not only did Canaris's department, Military Intelligence (the *Abwehr*) become absorbed into the SD in 1944, even the frontier police (*Grenzpolizei*) were claimed in their

Left: France. An internment camp for Jews near Pithiviers. *Above:* Heinrich Müller, head of the Gestapo

turn by the Gestapo. By the end of the war, accommodation in the Prinz Albrecht-Strasse had grown far too restricted to contain Himmler's inflated administration, and it eventually spread over some thirty-eight buildings in Berlin.

Within a decade, Himmler had risen from the charge of some 200 men to become absolute controller of all German police operations in the greater part of Europe. He was accountable to no one but Hitler himself, and by a decree of 1940, when he was forty years of age, he made every man in police service accountable only to himself, as head of the SS. Only Himmler, therefore, could in the end bring a member of the police force before a tribunal to account for his conduct, and this would be a special SS tribunal presided over by one of Himmler's SS judges. Except for Hitler himself, no Nazi leader exercised power equal to that assumed by Himmler, although he continued to avoid the limelight, as was his nature. In August 1943 he became Minister of the Interior and immediately transferred much of the Ministry's activities to his all-embracing RSHA. Himmler cherished his power secretly. He was still at heart the clerk-like recluse, whose middle-class conscience refused to let him take advantage of his position to salt away wealth or become, like Göring, a glittering prince. He remained content with his files, his overloaded desk, and his sense of being a bureaucrat of destiny, the absolute servant of an absolute master.

Gestapo methods of arrest and interrogation

Behind any arrest by the Gestapo lay the prospect of interrogation. The Gestapo existed to uncover subversion, not crime, and its procedure was different from that of the criminal police. One of the seeming mysteries linked with the Gestapo is why the more obvious members of the German resistance against Hitler, men long known for their subversive activities, such as Carl Goerdeler, were not picked up sooner than they were for interrogation. To leave such men at large, however, was part of the Gestapo technique; they had to estimate whether they would learn more by watching a suspect man meet his contacts than by isolating and questioning him. The tendency therefore was to lull the suspect into a false sense of security rather than to arrest him on the first breath of suspicion.

Once he was arrested and taken (if he were in Berlin) to Gestapo headquarters in Prinz Albrecht-Strasse, he was utterly without protection. Gestapo techniques of interrogation have received prominent treatment in books and films, with sadistic interrogators grilling their sweating prisoners under arc-lamps and gesturing thug-like torturers to apply the next grade of pain. In fact, the methods used were as varied as the men who used them, and as varied as the status of the prisoners and the circumstances of their 'crime' against the State made necessary. A prisoner such as Pastor Dietrich Bonhoeffer would be interrogated without direct torture, though confined in harsh circumstances over a period lasting from April 1943 until his final, hasty execution in Flossenbürg concentration camp in April 1945. If a prisoner was well-known and had an important file with his name attached to it which had come into Gestapo hands from other sources (implying that the prisoner might at some stage be reclaimed), he had a better chance of receiving more intelligent and less bestially brutal treatment than if he were unknown and absorbed into Gestapo hands under, say, the *Nacht und Nebel* decree. The Gestapo were quite capable of arresting people of comparatively little importance, interrogating them intensely but quite

uselessly without torture, and then letting them go.

They could, in fact, behave quite arbitrarily, as a result of their own human weaknesses – laziness might infect them as well as brutal energy, or sardonic humour and false bonhomie replace acts of sadism. But no one rose in the Gestapo out of consideration for his fellow men. A Gestapo man, at any rate one having authority in the examination of prisoners, would not reach his position without acquiring cold and ruthless techniques of enquiry. However, even the Gestapo could be circumspect, even perhaps enjoy the exercise of skill in interrogation, gradually breaking down a prisoner's will to resist over prolonged periods of time. Everything was done to catch the prisoner off his guard. For instance, straight questioning on an intellectual level might suddenly be interrupted by shock treatment, with shouting and insults.

But the medieval torturer might always be standing behind the door. The interrogators, men initially trained as career police investigators

or even as lawyers, did not normally apply the torture themselves. Unless it was a straight beating-up of a kind any Gestapo man worth his salt could carry out with his fists or with a truncheon, experts were usually called in to conduct the more scientific kinds of torture, for it must always be remembered that a person under interrogation was only of value to the Gestapo if he were in a fit condition to give up his information. Apart from being kicked or beaten, often surrounded by several men at once, a prisoner could be subjected to suspension by the arms which had been first tied behind his back; finger or toe nails could be wrenched up or torn away; the body could be burned with red-hot cigarette ends; prisoners could be stripped and tortured by electric shocks applied to the sensitive parts of their bodies; they could be held under cold water until their lungs reached bursting-point. After being revived, they might immediately be subjected to further torture. Women were not respected by their male torturers; they too were stripped, humiliated, and assaulted in

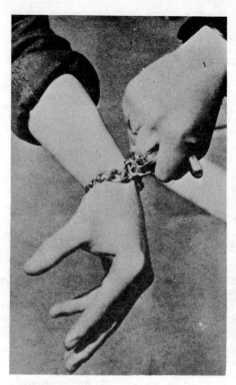
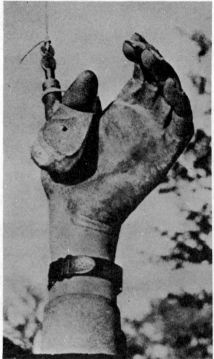

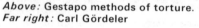

Above: Gestapo methods of torture.
Far right: Carl Gördeler

ways most likely to break them down.

Prisoners of great strength of mind would brace themselves to take the lacerations and the agonies which these bouts of pain inflicted, and learn how to relax momentarily during the intervals between the successive assaults upon their bodies. Or they would faint, after which they might be revived violently with a bucket of cold water. The very strong managed to resist such treatment, and true resistance meant keeping back essential information whatever agonies were devised to break a prisoner down.

Dr Fabian von Schlabrendorff, a member of the German resistance against Hitler who was taken prisoner after the failure of the attempt on the Führer's life in July 1944, has given a detailed account of the progressive tortures to which he was subjected at Gestapo headquarters in Berlin. Schlabrendorff, a man of great courage and clear mind under duress, brought a lawyer's skill to bear in resisting the assaults made by Habecker, his interrogator. He knew the tricks that would be used initially to break him – the pretended evidence against him in the file on the table, the contents of which he would not be allowed to see, the threats to his family and friends, the production of forged affidavits and the like. He was always ready in his cell for the sudden summons to face the harsh lights and the questioning at any time of night or day. He was kept fettered hand and foot in his cell; he was given utterly inadequate food. But he was steeled to deny all knowledge useful to the Gestapo; he hoped to achieve some form of stalemate. In a sense, it was he who had to wear Habecker down.

Eventually Habecker's team, which included a girl, got to work on him. Habecker himself struck him, and then incited the girl to do the same. Other interrogators used the sudden switch from blandishments to shouting abuse, an unnerving experience unless you are ready for this and keep

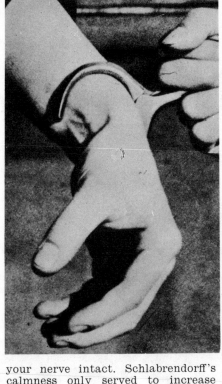

your nerve intact. Schlabrendorff's calmness only served to increase Habecker's anger, and he himself applied the first stage of real torture, chaining Schlabrendorff's hands behind his back and locking his fingers one by one in a vice which injected spikes into his finger-tips. Later he was strapped onto a frame, and a larger form of vice drove sharp points into his thighs and legs. Then he was strapped down onto a medieval stretching-frame, which wrenched the body slowly or expanded it in agonising jerks. A verbal barrage was kept up against him while he suffered. On each occasion he finally collapsed he was taken back to his cell to recover. On one occasion his body was soaked with blood, and he suffered a heart attack. He was surprised at his own endurance, and in the end, when he was contemplating suicide, he hit on the device of inventing a confession which could do no harm to anyone still alive. Immediately the tortures ceased. He had made a form of confession; this was all the Gestapo wanted. After this, he had to endure only

what all his fellow prisoners endured – starvation and sleeping in his cell whilst tightly shackled, with a harsh, naked light streaming down into his eyes.

The Gestapo, like the SS, were everywhere in German-controlled Europe. For example, in his book on the Gestapo, Jacques Delarue describes in particular the organisation of the secret police in France. Their full-scale operations extended to the whole of France during 1942, when they officially took over in the so-called free zone of Vichy France. The head office of the Gestapo was, naturally, based on Paris; the seventeen regional offices included centres at Bordeaux, Nancy, Rouen, Lyons, Marseilles, Montpellier, and Vichy itself, while they in turn controlled over fifty branch sections and over twenty frontier stations and posts. France was therefore covered by a closely organised network of Gestapo controls, including their commandos of killers, and active agents and collaborators infiltrating into every level of French society.

The Action Groups: from Poland to Russia

The Action Groups *(Einsatzgruppen)* were, as we have seen, reformed for the purpose of 'cleaning-up' German controlled Poland. The acquisition of Poland meant for Hitler a small though significant step in his geo-political re-ordering of Europe in favour of German unification, but it also meant responsibility for the fate of many millions of people he did not want. Mass-assassination conducted on a racial basis – genocide, as it came to be called – was initially disguised as the crushing of opposition.

It was no use expecting the German army to carry out this operation. Organized killing in cold blood cannot be entrusted to untrained men, conditioned only to killing within the recognized boundaries of warfare. It was Himmler's responsibility to assemble groups of men, relatively small in numbers, and send them in behind the army to act at once as security police and executioners wherever pockets of resistance could be found or, as policy dictated, were supposed to exist. Many senior officers in the army came back from Poland in a state of shock at what they had seen done by Himmler's SS commandos.

Hitler's invasion of Russia began on 22nd June 1941. Hitler was determined, if he could, to use *Blitzkrieg* methods to reach Moscow and Leningrad before the hard conditions of winter set in. Once again, the SS Action Groups were to follow in the wake of the army, this time with secret instructions to accomplish mass-genocide irrespective of any overt policy of 'security', though all the Jews encountered were usually classed as 'partisans' in the Action Group reports. Long before the invasion, in March 1941, Keitel, Hitler's Chief of Staff, signed an anticipatory order to the army commands responsible for the campaign against Russia, requiring them to provide the Action Groups with quarters, supplies, and transport. Though the German army did not normally take an active part in the killings, many knew perfectly well that they were taking place.

Four separate Action Groups were

set up, with a strength of between 500 and 1,000 men each. The total number needed for this work never exceeded 3,000. Within a few months it has been estimated they managed to exterminate a million people, and Raul Hilberg holds that as many as 1,400,000 Jews died as a result of the Action Groups and succeeding bodies of SS commandos by the spring of 1942.

It must not be forgotten that on 6th June 1941, Hitler had issued his *Kommissarbefehl*, the order giving effect to the murder of Red Army commissars; this was to be followed by orders given out at various intervals which led to the extermination by the SS not only of the political agents, the commissars, but of Russian prisoners-of-war in general, after large numbers of these had fallen into German hands, and so became classed, like the Jews, as unwanted people. The wholesale execution of Russian prisoners followed, leading into a complete pattern of extermination similar to that designed for the Jews. A High Command report dated 1st May 1944 gave the following statistics: total number of Red Army men taken prisoner-of-war, 5,165,381; two million deaths through 'wastage'; 280,000 officers and other ranks died or missing in transit camps; 1,030,157 shot while trying to escape or sent to concentration camps. Approaching three and a half million Russian soldiers died while in German hands, and mainly in the hands of the SS, if 'wastage' can be taken to refer, in part at least, to the initial exterminations. The army itself, however, cannot escape some guilt in playing its part in this barbaric slaughter.

To German-occupied Poland's population of some two million Jews Russia was to add some five million, of whom four-fifths lived in the area so soon to be occupied by Germany, including the area of Poland originally taken over by Russia herself, where Poland's remaining 1,350,000 Jews were caught by surprise when the Germans suddenly arrived. In the Ukraine, invaded by Germany in July, over one and a half million Russian Jews were threatened with

Village massacres by the SS in Russia were common practice

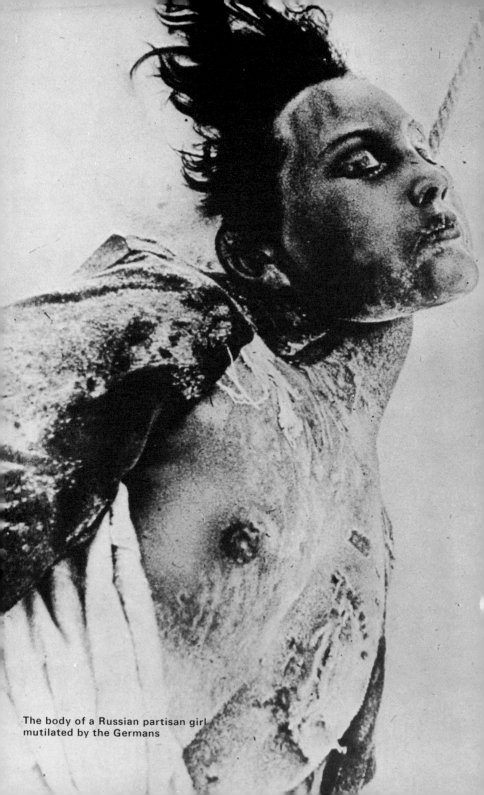

The body of a Russian partisan girl
mutilated by the Germans

extinction. In the end, one and a half million somehow managed to move east away from the Nazis, but several million remained helpless in German hands in both occupied eastern Poland and in Russia.

The work of the Action Groups is well-documented; many of their reports to headquarters survive, and were used during the post-war trials; they were as meticulous as they were detailed. For example, Action Group A claimed to have killed 125,000 Jews by 15th October 1941; Group B claimed 45,000 dead by 14th November (with more to come later when their statistics were more complete); Group C scored 75,000 by 3rd November; and Group D reached 55,000 dead by 12th December. This gave a total of some 300,000 dead through extermination during the opening months of the campaign. Action Group A went so far as to claim they had received active help from the army, but this was abnormal. Typical of the Action Group reports are the following, sent in from the Kiev sector:

'In collaboration with the Group staff and two Kommandos of the Police Regiment South, the Sonderkommando 4a executed on 29th and 30th September 33,771 Jews. Money, valuables, underwear and clothing were secured and placed at the disposal of the NSV [Nazi Party Welfare Organization] for the use of racial Germans, or given to the city administration authorities for use by the needy population. The transaction was carried out without friction. No incidents occurred. The 'resettlement measure' against the Jews was approved throughout by the population. The fact that in reality the Jews were liquidated was hardly known until now; according to up-to-date experience, it would, however, hardly have been objected to. The measures were also approved by the army.'

And the following month:
'The difficulties resulting from such a large-scale action . . . were overcome in Kiev by requesting the Jewish population through wall posters to move. Although only 5,000 to 6,000 Jews had been expected at first, more than 30,000 arrived who until the very moment of their execution still believed in their resettlement, thanks to extremely clever organization . . . Approximately 75,000 Jews have been liquidated in this manner.'

In charge of one of these Action Groups was the young intellectual from Hanover who has already been mentioned – Professor Otto Ohlendorf, the man whom Himmler had regarded as an unsoldierly academic. Like others of his kind, he was to prove more coldly ruthless than men with a less disciplined mentality. Sensitivity and a humane conscience are not necessarily to be found in all men of intellectual capacity. People who knew Ohlendorf have said that he was essentially a cold man, rather vain and given to theoretical argument, using involved, academic terminology. He was, however, proud of his rank of SS-General, which he achieved when he accepted leadership of an Action Group. He was not unique; the Action Groups' senior officers were mostly young professional men.

Ohlendorf, however, had at least one good quality – considerable frankness when he was put on trial after the War. He made no attempt to hide what he had done.

Ohlendorf: 'Mr Prosecutor . . . I considered the order wrong, but I was under military coercion and carried it out . . . knowing that . . . the measures were ordered as emergency measures in self-defence. The order, as such, even now, I consider to have been wrong, but there is no question for me whether it was moral or immoral, because a leader who has to deal with such serious questions decides on his own responsibility. This is his responsibility. I cannot examine and I cannot judge; I am not entitled to do so.'

Prosecuting Counsel: 'You surrendered your moral conscience to Adolf Hitler, did you not?'

Ohlendorf: 'No. But I surrendered my moral conscience to the fact that I was a soldier, and therefore a cog in a low position, relatively, of a great machine. And what I did there is the same as is done in any other Army. As a soldier I got an order, and I obeyed this order as a soldier.'

Prosecuting Counsel: 'You refuse to express a moral judgment?'

Ohlendorf: 'Yes.'

An execution in Poland. The firing squad are German soldiers not SS

He described how Himmler visited his group in Nikolaev and reinforced the need for genocide:

Ohlendorf: 'The situation in Nikolaev was especially depressing in the moral sense because, in agreement with the army, we had excluded a large number of the Jews, the farmers, from the execution. When the Reichsführer SS was in Nikolaev on 4th or 5th October, I was reproached for this measure and he ordered that henceforth, even against the will of the army, the executions should take place as planned . . . . He added that he alone would carry the responsibility . . . . None of the men would bear any of the responsibility, but he demanded the execution of this order, even though he knew how harsh these measures were. Nevertheless, after supper, I spoke to the Reichsführer and I pointed out the inhuman burden

which was being imposed on the men in killing all these civilians. I didn't even get an answer.'

He told, too, how the massacres were normally carried out: 'The unit selected for this task would enter a village or city and order the prominent Jewish citizens to call together all Jews for the purpose of resettlement. They were requested to hand over their valuables to the leaders of the unit and shortly before the execution to surrender their outer cloth-ing. The men, women and children were led to a place of execution which in most cases was located next to a more deeply excavated anti-tank ditch. Then they were shot kneeling or standing, and the corpses thrown into the ditch. I never permitted the shooting by individuals in Group D, but ordered that several men should shoot at the same time to avoid direct personal responsibility.'

The Action Groups were in time winnowed down to the hardened killers in the field, but not without some difficulty. Even though these men were ceaselessly brainwashed and regarded all Jews as vermin, they had quite normally to be heated up with alcohol before going about their duties. One SS General, Bach-Zelewski, himself suffered from severe nervous disorder, and so did many men serving in the Action Groups. Even Himmler, on one of the rare excursions from his desk to the actual front where his orders were being carried out, was, according to Bach-Zelewski, who was present, visibly upset by what he had to see. Bach-Zelewski, a favoured officer, turned on him and said: 'Look at the eyes of the men in this commando, how deeply shaken they are. These men are finished for the rest of their lives. What kind of followers are we training here? Either neurotics or savages.' Himmler admitted the work was terrible (he used the word *widerlich*, repulsive), and he hated it all as much as they did. But, he added inevitably, Hitler's orders must be obeyed. He, as *Reichsführer SS*, was responsible before God and Hitler for what was being done.

The German Action Groups and the SS were not working alone. As soon as the practice of virulent anti-Semitism became official, there were a number of willing hands ready to assist in the mass killing. The extreme right-wing Iron Guards in Rumania, for example, conducted genocide campaigns against the Jews of Bessarabia. These helpless groups of Jews fled hither and thither in the search of some place of shelter. Many paid inordinate sums to escape in unseaworthy ships to Palestine, only to be turned away by the mandatory authority, the British, who were determined to prevent all forms of illegal entry and keep the number of immigrants down to the permitted total of 75,000 only during the first five years of the 1940s.

This story of Jewish suffering must never be forgotten. The Action Groups fulfilled the first major part in the campaign of genocide which was about to be developed scientifically by the SS in the extermination camps established by Himmler on Polish soil. If this agony undergone by the Jews of central Europe during the 1940s is lost to mind by those who never experienced it or witnessed it, one reason is the utter lack of comprehension of such things by civilized people. When the stories of mass killings began to leak out, as they inevitably had to, both Germany and the outside world supplied another form of resistance to the truth – that of blank unbelief. Himmler's greatest

ally at home and abroad proved to be this sheer incomprehension, and the silent rejection of such evidence as reached normal German or foreign hands. The general public refused to accept any evidence offered as one of the less healthy fantasies of wartime rumour.

Few believed that men and women could be trained in sufficient numbers to undertake the mass-murder of innocent people. Only after the war did Germany and the rest of the world begin to face the killers and see what kind of men and women had been recruited by the SS into this brotherhood of blood. They came, in fact, from every walk of life. Some of them are still being tried today in West Germany.

Himmler reviews Waffen SS units

The SS and the outright policy of genocide

The need for genocide, more especially of the European Jews and 'unacceptable' Slavs, might be said to have overtaken the Nazi leaders by the onrush of events. It became, therefore, the 'final solution'. There was for a brief while a hare-brained scheme in Himmler's mind to seize Madagascar and people it with Europe's Jews. But it had disappeared by 1941.

Absolute power soon breeds absolute contempt for the powerless. Why waste time, space, and money on any 'unwanted' people – imbeciles, for instance, hopeless cripples, the aged, the geriatric? They only act as a drag to the healthy progress of the State. Late in 1939, Himmler had received a highly secret directive from Philip Bouhler, head of Hitler's Chancellery, that all incurables in German mental hospitals were to undergo euthanasia. Hitler had sent a written note to Bouhler to that effect during October of that year. The SS were to supply the doctors to carry out this programme of 'mercy-killing', which was to be performed at selected extermination centres operating under guard. Doctors, nurses, and ambulance men had to be briefed. The relatives of the selected patients were to be left uninformed until they received a notification of death which falsified the cause. Some 60,000 patients died in this way before public protest, largely organized through the churches, led to the operation being stopped by Hitler himself in August 1941. By that time there was other work for the SS doctors to undertake, and euthanasia of the unfit was confined to the concentration camps.

Dr Karl Brandt, who was in charge of the euthanasia scheme, gave evidence during the celebrated Doctors' Trial in Nuremberg begun in 1946. He showed no compunction for his actions: 'It may seem to have been inhuman. . . . The underlying motive was the desire to help individuals who could not help themselves. . . . Such considerations cannot be regarded as inhuman. Nor did I ever feel it to be in any degree unethical or immoral. . . . I am convinced that if Hippocrates were alive today he would change the

Karl Brandt on trial at Nuremberg　　**Dr Mengele**

wording of his Oath . . . in which a doctor is forbidden to administer poison to an invalid even upon demand. . . . I have a perfectly clear conscience about the part I played in the affair.'

The SS doctors numbered in the end some 350, and many of them were directly involved in the concentration camps. Already, in 1939, work had begun, too, on what was to become the most horrifying contribution of the SS medical teams to the genocide operation – the so-called medical tests. These started with the use of prisoners for testing the effect of liquid war gases, mustard and phosgene, when applied to the human skin; symptoms were recorded and photographed, and the prisoners eventually died in gradually increasing agony. These tests were carried out over a period of years, at one stage under the supervision of a professor of anatomy who held a senior rank in the SS.

Himmler regarded this work as entirely justifiable, and soon the tests escalated until any SS doctor in a position of reasonable authority could order whatever human samples he wished. The Natzweiler concentration camp authorities even tried to make a trade out of selling prisoners for experiments, but normally an order from Himmler's office was sufficient for doctors 'recognised' as experimenters to be supplied with

prisoners. The key period for these experiments spanned 1941-44.

Dr Sigmund Rascher, formerly of the Luftwaffe and later of the SS, received Himmler's permission to have prisoners put at his disposal for low pressure, high altitude experiments. The message he received from Himmler's secretary was: 'I can inform you that prisoners will, of course, be gladly made available for the high flight researches.' Low pressure chambers were established in Dachau concentration camp, and Rascher worked his way through some 200 prisoners, of whom seventy died as a result of his research methods. Rascher's experiments, which also included the effects of freezing on the human body, were considered worthless and utterly unscientific even by Himmler's key medical adviser, Professor Gebhardt. One of Rascher's assistants was among the defendants at the Doctors' Trial. When questioned about the legality of what he had done, this was all he had to say: 'I had no scruples on legal grounds. For I knew that the man who had officially authorised these experiments was Himmler . . . In the sphere of what one may call medical ethics it was rather different. It was a wholly new experience for us all to be offered persons to be experimented upon . . . I had to get used to the idea.'

Himmler was later to regret his

patronage of Rascher, when it was learned that even his children were bogus. Himmler had been impressed when he heard that Rascher's mistress had added to the Führer's population at the late age of forty-eight, and he had stood as pagan 'god-parent' to the children, who were later discovered to have been abducted. Rascher's experiments degenerated into the revolting farce of confining men for a period in water a few degrees above freezing, and then using camp prostitutes to 'warm' them back to life. These experiments were conducted on the grounds that they were vital to the Luftwaffe, and they went on until Rascher was himself placed under arrest for abduction. He was shot at Dachau before it was liberated in 1945.

Himmler, however, was obsessed by the idea of these human experiments, and Gebhardt, as his closest medical adviser, began experiments himself which led up to the infection of Polish women prisoners, who were already ear-marked to die, with gas-gangrenous wounds. One of the medical men concerned in this work said during the Doctors' Trial: 'I believed we were offering reasonable chances of survival to the subjects of our experiments, who were living under German law and could not otherwise escape the death penalty. . . . I was not then a doctor in civil life, free to take his own decisions. I was . . . a medical expert bound to act in exactly the same way as a soldier under discipline.'

Worst of all the experiments, however, and the ones conducted on the largest scale, were attempts to discover some system for mass-sterilisation, so that whole populations might be easily and cheaply wiped out within a single generation. Many means were tried with a cruelly haphazard, amateur enthusiasm by a number of alleged medical men, sometimes 'qualified' and sometimes not. Abortive attempts were made to sterilise by means of drugs, by X-rays applied to the genitals, and by injecting acids into the uterus. Men and women died in agony with the most sensitive areas of their bodies burned and raw. The experiments multiplied over the years – for instance, in typhus and

epidemic hepatitis virus 'research'. Spare-part surgery was introduced, and the limbs of prisoners were stolen and given to Gebhardt's patients in the sanatorium near Ravensbrück where he practised, and where Himmler occasionally retired for rest and cures for his chronic stomach complaint.

Although some 350 doctors of German stock worked for the SS, only a small proportion of these were directly involved in the experiments. What is alarming is that the moral sense of conduct towards fellow human beings should have been abandoned by so many men whose profession was entirely concerned with their welfare. The most pernicious aspect of Himmler's indoctrination was that it dulled the basic sense of the distinction between right and wrong in those who took service in the SS. Nowhere is this more apparent than in the case of the SS doctors.

All such experiments on living human beings were, of course, criminal, and in a similar category of crime was the use of prisoners, usually freshly killed for the purpose, to supply evidence for the 'researches' in the special race investigation department set up within the SS Institute for Research and Study of Heredity (the *Ahnenerbe*), the organisation designed to lend an aura of science to Himmler's utterly unscientific prejudices. One of the research departments of the Institute began to collect the skulls of Jews in large numbers in order that the characteristics of this branch of what the Nazis termed sub-humanity should be studied and re-studied. 'Consignments' of Jews and Jewesses were constantly being sent; the bodies on one occasion at least were noticed by a witness to be still warm.

In Auschwitz, the criminal doctor Fritz Mengele turned himself into an amateur pathologist whose hobby was the study of twins, in the hope that he might discover the secret of dual and multiple births so that good German mothers might always have more than one child by each pregnancy. Everyone was pressed into service to discover twins among the incoming prisoners, who were then studied, first alive and later dead, while the elegant and cynical Mengele compiled his sheaf of beautifully typed and entirely useless notes.

Only a single, somewhat more positive aspect emerged from the macabre horror of these racial obsessions and researches: the SS *Lebensborn* maternity homes, established before the war. These were widely extended in wartime, and mothers of suitable stock were assured of a peaceful and well-attended childbirth, whether their children were legitimate or illegitimate. But even here, Himmler's fads managed to penetrate. Orders survive instructing the women to eat porridge on the grounds that it was the food that produced the lean and hardy Scots, who were among the ideal Nordic types Himmler most favoured. But the women did not like the idea; they thought the porridge would make them fat.

However, the life harboured in the *Lebesborn* homes was as nothing to the huge losses inflicted once genocide became recognised Nazi practice.

One of Dr Rascher's experiments. Prisoner in the low-pressure chamber

The development from enforced, mass-euthanasia carried out in secret by SS doctors and nurses to mass-genocide can be placed at early in 1941 – that is, the period when Hitler was preparing the ground for the invasion of Russia.

It is true that in a speech made as early as January 1939, Hitler had made an open threat of extermination of the Jews. As usual, this was taken as the exaggeration of rhetoric, if it were noted at all at the time: 'If internationally financed Jewry inside and outside Europe should succeed once more in plunging nations into another world war, the consequence will not be the Bolshevization of the earth and thereby the victory of Jewry, but the annihilation [*Vernichtung*] of the Jewish race in Europe'.

The first steps taken towards the planned extermination of the European Jews who lay in the path of Hitler's progress to the east came with the establishment of Auschwitz as the future headquarters for genocide. This concentration camp had been set up initially in June 1940, with Hoess as its commandant, a

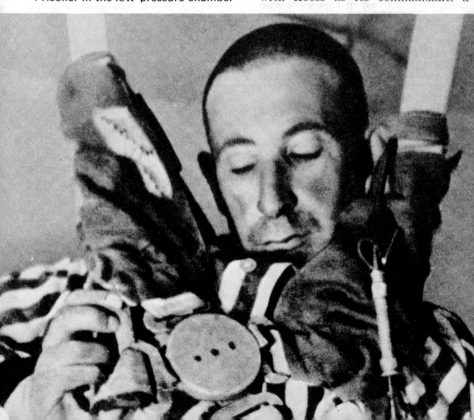

considerable position of trust for a man who only a few years before had been a newly-recruited, trainee guard at Dachau. After the war, Hoess admitted receiving his orders from Himmler in May 1941. His signed statement reads: 'I personally arranged on orders received from Himmler in May 1941 the gassing of two million persons between June-July 1941 and the end of 1943, during which time I was Commandant of Auschwitz.' Hoess was proud enough of his achievements to produce statistics whenever the opportunity arose, as it did (to the horror of everyone, prosecutors, press, public, and most of the defendants alike) when he gave evidence at the Nuremberg trial. In addition, as we have seen, he wrote his memoirs while in captivity. 'By the will of the Reichsführer SS,' he wrote, 'Auschwitz became the greatest human extermination centre of all time.'

Meanwhile, the High Command was warned to keep themselves clear of any direct involvement in the activities of the SS. There was to be no repetition of the interference that had taken place in Poland. 'The Reichsführer SS shall act independently and under his own responsibility', said Hitler in a written order issued in March. In the same month, Himmler called a conference of very senior SS officers at which, according to one witness, Bach-Zelewski, he spoke of the future decimation of the Slav population by thirty million. This too appears to have been taken as a rhetorical exaggeration. But exaggeration of what?

The extermination programme was placed in the direct charge of a combination of SS officers who received authority for what they did directly from Hitler or, on Hitler's behalf, through Himmler. Whatever he might try to say subsequently in his defence at Nuremberg, there can be little doubt that Göring was implicated as well. It was he who, again on Hitler's behalf, passed on to Heydrich the actual order which made use of the notorious, veiled term for extermination, *Endlösung*, or 'final solution'. The use of veiled terms of this kind, such as 'special treatment' and 'resettlement' in written directives and in the formal minutes of conferences was adopted deliberately in order to keep knowledge of the policy of active extermination to as restricted a circle as possible.

Although Jews, along with other Polish civilians had been shot in large numbers by the Action Groups in Poland, there appears to have been no written order to kill them. The orders had been solely to round up and deport the Jews and arrest 'subversive' elements in the Polish population. Heydrich, however, had spoken at the time of the movement of the Jews as an 'interim measure' prior to some undefined 'top secret "final objective" which would take rather longer to achieve'. No one can do more now than guess at what this meant – perhaps at this stage no more than segregation in a controlled area of central Europe, or even Himmler's old idea of Madagascar as a Jewish ghetto. In any case, apart from the few thousands who had to do the job, no one wanted to know what only too many half-realized was in fact going on. The suppression of knowledge, like the suppression of conscience, became only too evident in large numbers of people. Nazism dulled the moral sense. Extermination was to be the best-kept 'psychlogical' secret of the war, both inside and outside Germany.

The search for written orders initiating genocide continues. There is one involving executions sent by Heydrich to the Action Group commanders and dated 2nd July 1941, this preceding by almost a month the celebrated order sent to him by Göring. A section of this reads: 'The following will be executed: all officials of the Comintern (most of these will certainly be career politicians): officials of senior and middle rank and "extremists" in the Party, the central committee, and the provincial and district committees: the Peoples' Commissars: *Jews in the service of the Party or the State;* other extremist elements. . . . No steps will be taken to interfere with any purges that may be initiated by anti-Communist or anti-Jewish elements in the newly occupied territories. On the contrary, these are to be *secretly encouraged.*'

The only evidence as yet that some orders were issued (most probably verbally) to 'eliminate' Jews, without any covering reference to their being officials or partisans, comes from the subsequent references in the Action Group reports, in which statistics are given (as we have seen) of the number of Jews rounded up and shot 'in accordance with basic instructions'. Russian Jews were being executed during 1941 and 1942 in their hundreds of thousands.

Göring's order to Heydrich of 31st July 1941, given him with Himmler's knowledge, has been translated as follows: 'Supplementing the task that was assigned to you on 24th January 1939, to solve the Jewish problem by means of emigration and evacuation in the best possible way according to present conditions, I herewith instruct you to make all necessary preparations as regards organisational, financial and material matters for a total solution [*Gesamtlösung*] of the Jewish question within the area of German influence in Europe. . . . I instruct you further to submit to me as soon as possible a general plan showing the measure for organisation and for action necessary to carry out the desired final solution [*Endlösung*] of the Jewish question.'

Göring was to maintain at Nuremberg that this order for a 'final solution' meant no more than deportation and a just confiscation of their ill-gotten property for the benefit of the Reich. But the notorious 'Green File' directives, composed at Göring's order during the middle months of 1941 in preparation for the Russian campaign, were also produced in evidence against him. In these it was coldly set down that 'many tens of millions of people in this area [that is, Soviet territory] . . . will become redundant and will either die or have to emigrate to Siberia.' People in the Ukraine as well as the north would be faced with starvation as Göring plundered their granaries and transported the food back to Germany. 'I intend to plunder and to do it thoroughly,' said Göring at the time. As early as 20th May 1941, there are

references in an RSHA decree circulated in France and Belgium to a communication received from Göring concerning the movement of Jews, and referring twice to, 'the certain final solution of the Jewish problem'. Göring had been among those present at a Führer conference on 16th July at which Hitler had spoken openly of 'shootings, deportations and so on' in order to clear 'the whole vast area' for 'the protection of the administration'. 'The best way,' Hitler had added, 'is to shoot anyone who so much as looks like giving trouble.' Göring's order of 31st July to Heydrich therefore appears to be the formal confirmation of much that had been well understood verbally, and not an entirely new order initiating extermination as official policy.

It is of some significance that Heydrich received this order direct from Göring, and not through Himmler. Heydrich, only ten years before a cashiered naval lieutenant, was now recognized by Hitler as a man of ruthless capacity, and in certain respects superior even to Himmler. Hitler had already marked him out, and the following September he was appointed Acting Reich Protector in Czechoslovakia, that is, Hitler's supreme representative in an important territory where there was growing unrest and active resistance under the weak administration of Baron Constantin von Neurath. Heydrich was promoted an SS-General, and held in effect the rank of a minister. He was thirty-seven. It would seem, in the inevitable rat-race which characterised Nazi Germany, that this promotion alarmed Himmler. His paternal affection for Heydrich was not sufficient for him to relish his subordinate acquiring any form of independent power. According to such witnesses as Schellenberg (a shrewd, if somewhat unreliable observer), Himmler was afraid of Heydrich because he was so dependent upon the man's ceaseless energy in seeing the worst tasks assigned to the SS were in fact carried out. It was probably as much a relief as it was a sorrow to Himmler when Heydrich was assassinated in Prague the following year. Schellenberg, who disliked Heydrich while at the same time

Heydrich as Acting Reichsprotektor, Czechoslovakia

105

acknowledging the force of his personality, used the removal of this dangerous superior officer to supplant him in Himmler's esteem. Schellenberg's extraordinary influence upon Himmler began in 1942, and was to a certain extent to seduce him from his absolute loyalty to Hitler.

Heydrich's additional responsibilities made him, in turn, more dependent upon subordinates. His appointment in Prague was supplementary to his duties as controller of the secret extermination programme. In any case, Heydrich was most unwilling to cut himself off from Berlin, and it would seem likely he only welcomed his new appointment in Prague because of the high form of promotion and independent status it afforded him. An aircraft normally stood by to allow him to commute between Prague and Berlin. However, as a dynamic young man of action, what he most needed was a highly efficient aide to take full responsibility on his behalf for the administrative problems of genocide. Heydrich found this man in another Himmler-like bureaucrat, the 'Jewish specialist' at SS headquarters, Adolf Eichmann.

It was Eichmann, therefore, who organised on Heydrich's behalf the notorious Wannsee Conference, the lakeside meeting which took place on 20th January 1942. The minutes of the 'top secret' discussion survive, carefully phrased in veiled language. Although Himmler was not there – the conference was on the level of senior officials – the ministries most involved in the control of the eastern territories were all represented. After the war, certain of these officials had good reason to be sorry they had been detailed to attend; it made them party to discussions which implied the crime of genocide.

Heydrich presided; he described himself as Göring's 'commissioner for the preparation of the final solution of the European Jewish problem.' Göring, he said, must be kept informed how the matter was being organised. He went on: 'Undoubtedly a great part will fall out through natural diminution [natürliche Verminderung]. The remnant that is finally able to survive all this – since

this is undoubtedly the section with the strongest resistance – must be treated accordingly, since these people, representing a natural selection, are to be regarded as the germ cell of a new Jewish development. See the experience of history.'

Details of what was to happen to the Jews in each specific area were then discussed, largely in terms of the movement of populations, their fitness for work, and the 'final solution' for those millions who were held to be useless to the Reich. The word extermination, or its equivalent, was naturally never used, and this was the pretence on which those present fell back when interrogated after the war. 'I cannot remember the final solution having been discussed in the sense attributed to that term,' said one, while another, more frank than his former colleague, admitted, 'it was so horrible that no one properly spoke about it'.

Other conferences followed the one which took place in January; at these, attended in March and October by more junior officials, Eichmann himself presided. By October he was responsible directly to Himmler, for Heydrich was now dead. At these meetings he described enthusiastically the experiments being undertaken by the SS doctors to secure mass-sterilisation. Soon the Jews were to suffer at Eichmann's hands; he was to be responsible for organising the mass-movement to the labour and extermination camps.

By 1941, the SS might be said to be concentrating on three main fields of activity, almost all of them by now submerged beneath the level of open, public knowledge. These were, maintenance of security by means of the SD and the Gestapo throughout Germany and occupied Europe, the exploitation of forced labour, and the development, through the extermination camps, of a gradually accelerating operation of genocide. Of all this, the most significant to history was the construction and operation of the wartime concentration camps both for the exploitation of slave-labour and for extermination, activities which overlapped, since the slaves were for the most part regarded as expendable and rapidly worked

Prisoners using picks to break clay at Sachsenhausen in 1941

to death. Once the Jews, the unwanted Slavs, the Gypsies and the Russian prisoners-of-war were secure inside the camps so hurriedly extended to contain them, a large measure of secrecy could be imposed on what was going on. It was the duty of the SS to develop every sanction which they could to ensure a maximum security screen for the movement of prisoners mostly across considerable distances on their journey to the camps. They travelled as special 'consignments', crowded into cattle-trucks and other forms of enclosed railway wagons. Since both the SS and the Gestapo were expert in security, and their reputation inspired so much fear, they were largely successful in maintaining their screen of silence, although a total of millions were being transported by rail to Auschwitz-Birkenau, Treblinka, and the other extermination centres.

A specialised branch of the SS was, as we have seen, concerned with the economic exploitation of these slave-workers. The farming out of the vast resources of labour grew into a major undertaking. The presence of forced labour, in any case, became accepted everywhere; deported Polish workers, for example, might be found all over Germany, replacing German farm-labourers, and working quietly with little more supervision than a tolerant German farmer himself provided. Such men were fortunate, since they were often well treated, except that they received no wage. Less fortunate prisoners worked as organised gangs on road construction, fortifications, and the like, and were often transported to western Europe – to France, or even the Channel Islands. As far as the SS were directly concerned in this exploitation, in which the whole German economy was engaged, Oswald Pohl, the former paymaster in the German navy, represented Himmler. The task became so great that Pohl acquired a staff of some 1,500. Pohl soon found that his duties were in direct opposition to the extermination programme, but the camp system soon became organised at least as much for the use of slave-labour as for outright, immediate extermination.

Himmler was enthusiastic about the profits which were to be made by hiring out forced labour. Firms, especially those engaged in war work, were encouraged to apply to the SS Main Economic Office if they were in need of unskilled labour. The charge was between four and eight marks a day for each man employed, according to the measure of his usefulness; the cost of maintenance of prisoners was officially estimated at as little as thirty pfennigs a day, since they were clothed in worthless rags and given in the way of food far less than the bare necessities of life. If they died at work, it scarcely mattered. New consignments of prisoners were constantly arriving, and had for a brief while a higher level of energy. It is to the lasting shame of such great firms as Siemens, I G Farben, and Krupp that they readily accepted the use of this form of labour, and even constructed special plants near the camps in order to exploit it. Himmler even planned to set up his own SS controlled factories.

The following account, given in testimony during the Nuremberg trial, shows how the prisoners were treated: 'The camp inmates were mostly Jewish women and girls from Hungary and Rumania . . . brought to Essen at the beginning of 1944 and put to work at Krupp's. The accommodation and feeding of the camp prisoners were of a low standard. . . . The daily working period was of ten to eleven hours. Although the prisoners were completely undernourished, their work was very heavy physically. The prisoners were often ill-treated at their work benches by Nazi overseers and female SS guards. At five or six o'clock in the afternoon they were marched back to camp. The accompanying guards consisted of female SS who, in spite of the protests from the civilian population, often ill-treated the prisoners on the way back, kicking and hitting them and abusing them in foul language. . . . At six or seven in the evening these exhausted people arrived back in camp. Then the real midday meal was distributed. This consisted of cabbage soup. This was followed by the evening meal of watery soup and a piece of bread which was for the following day. Occasionally the food on Sundays was better. As long as it existed there was never any inspection of the camp by members of the firm of Krupp.'

Himmler was determined to build up the resources of the SS against the great future which lay before them once the war was won. Although his visits to the concentration camps during the war were strictly limited, when he did visit Auschwitz, in March 1941, his principal concern was with its economic development, not with the extermination programme. He came to survey the prospects for housing labour for I G Farben's synthetic rubber factory. Later, in 1942, he paid a second visit, and on this occasion decided to watch the 'processing' (extermination) of a group of Jewish captives. It nauseated him.

Himmler, therefore, confined his personal link with genocide to such allusions as he chose to make in speeches before closed audiences made up of responsible SS officers or Nazi officials. Here he could speak with utter ruthlessness, and his words, like those already quoted on this subject, have become a part of Nazi history: 'What happens to a Russian or to a Czech does not interest me in the slightest. What the nations can offer in the way of good blood of our type, we will take, if necessary by kidnapping their children and raising them here with us. Whether nations live in prosperity or starve to death interests me only in so far as we need them for slaves of our *Kultur*. . . . Whether 10,000 Russian females fall down from exhaustion digging an anti-tank ditch interests me only in so far as the anti-tank ditch for Germany is finished. . . . We had to deal with the question: what about the women and the children? . . . I would not feel entitled merely to root out the men – well, let's call a spade a spade, for "root out" say kill or cause to be killed – well I just couldn't risk merely killing the man and allowing the children to grow up as avengers facing our sons and grandsons. We were forced to come to the grim decision that this people must be made to disappear from the face of the earth.'

In private, as Felix Kersten, his

Felix Kersten, Himmler's masseur and confidant towards the end of the war

masseur, has testified in his published memoirs, he was deeply disturbed by what had to be done. The nervous affliction of his youth, causing cramp of the stomach muscles, became chronic. Only Kersten's touch could relieve him, and so Kersten became Himmler's father-confessor during the middle years of the war, when he was virtually his patient's prisoner. 'It is the curse of greatness,' said Himmler, according to Kersten, 'that it must step over dead bodies to create new life.' He sustained himself with the traditional dream of a pan-Germanic imperialism, a Europe controlled by the Reich, together with a world colonial system modelled on the British Empire. Himmler apparently did not omit God from this scheme. He told Kersten that 'some higher Being . . . is behind nature. . . . If we refused to recognise that we should be no better than the Marxists. . . . I insist that members of the SS must believe in God.'

Auschwitz: slave-labour and extermination

Himmler's empire was the SS itself, and the concentration camp system, with its vast yield of wealth not only from the sale of labour, but from the theft of property from the incoming civilian prisoners. By the middle years of the war, the camps had greatly increased in numbers and were spread, mainly over Germany and Poland, in a network of principal centres, subsidiaries and labour outposts. In Poland, counting the smallest subsidiaries, there were over 400 camp centres, including some eighteen transit and evacuation camps for Poles intended to be sent west as slave labour and camps for prisoners serving short sentences.

At the heart of the Polish camp system were the seven extermination centres – Auschwitz-Birkenau, Maidanek, Stutthof, Chelmno, Belzec, Sobibor, and Treblinka. None of these camps were to attain the appalling efficiency of Auschwitz-Birkenau, which in any case was intended to become the largest centre of all, both for labour and extermination. Nevertheless, the others extermi-nated between them some two million people. Treblinka, covering thirty-three acres near Warsaw, alone accounted for some three-quarters of a million dead before it was closed down following a revolt of prisoners in August 1943 which was sufficiently successful for a large number to have escaped, killing more than a dozen SS guards. Hoess, on an official visit to Treblinka in 1941, kept his eye on his watch as he witnessed the slow asphixiation of victims in a gas-wagon – a form of despatch which, in his estimation, took far too long. This was no way in which to conduct efficient mass-murder. Soon enough Auschwitz was to be firmly established as the SS headquarters of death.

Only Eichmann and Ohlendorf have equalled Hoess in the frankness and detail of their revelations on the witness-stand. Hoess was found by the American prison psychologists to have developed a completely apathetic, matter-of-fact attitude to what he had done; had he not appeared so remote, lacking any kind

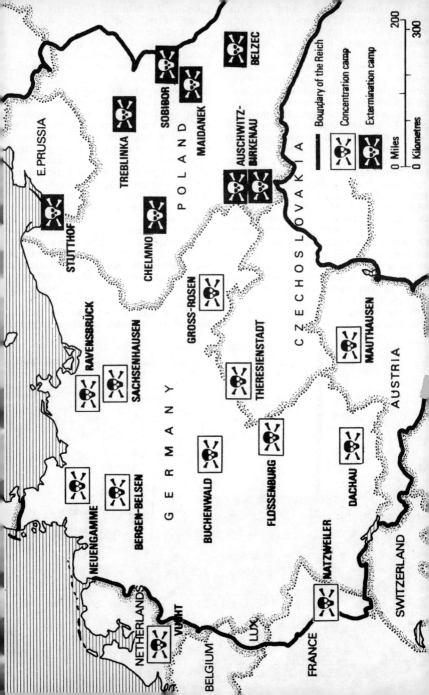

of emotional involvement in what he said, he might have been thought proud still of his efficiency. His statements at Nuremberg were delivered in a courtroom which became still with horror as all those listening tried to grasp the significance of the facts about the extermination camps, so long concealed or, when partially known, rejected as impossible. Some of Hoess's statements to the court took the form of testimony previously recorded and read aloud as he stood listening, ready to give his assent to the truth of his words:

Colonel Amen (American prosecuting counsel, quoting Hoess): 'When I set up the extermination building at Auschwitz, I used Zyclon B, which was a crystallised prussic acid which we dropped into the death-chamber from a small opening. It took from 3 to 15 minutes to kill the people in the death-chamber, depending on climatic conditions. We knew when the people were dead because their screaming stopped. We usually waited about half-an-hour before we opened the doors and removed the bodies. After the bodies were removed our special commandos took off the rings and extracted the gold teeth of the corpses."

'Is that true and correct, witness?'
Hoess: 'Yes.'

Amen: "Another improvement we made as compared with Treblinka was that we built our gas-chamber to accommodate 2,000 people at one time whereas at Treblinka their ten gas-chambers only accommodated 200 people each. The way we selected our victims was as follows: we had two SS doctors on duty at Auschwitz to examine the incoming transports of prisoners. The prisoners would be marched past one of the doctors who would make 'spot' decisions as they walked by. Those who were fit for work were sent into the camp. Others were sent immediately to the extermination plants. Children of tender years were invariably exterminated since, by reason of their youth, they were unable to work. At Treblinka the victims almost always knew that they were to be exterminated. We followed a better policy at Auschwitz by endeavouring to fool the victims into thinking that they were to go

through a delousing process. Of course, frequently they realized our true intentions and we sometimes had riots and difficulties due to that fact. Very frequently women would hide their children under their clothes but of course when we found them we would send the children in to be exterminated. We were required to carry out these exterminations in secrecy but naturally the foul and nauseating stench from the continuous burning of bodies permeated the entire area and all the people living in the surrounding districts knew that exterminations were going on at Auschwitz."

'Is all that true and correct, witness?'
Hoess: 'Yes.'

In order to carry out this work and bring it to the highest possible level of efficiency, Hoess claims in his prison memoirs that he became a changed man. 'I became a different person in Auschwitz. . . . I hedged myself in, became unapproachable, visibly harder. . . . Even people who hardly knew me felt sorry for me. . . . Alcohol, more than anything else, was able to put me into a happy and contented frame of mind.'

In court, however, he maintained his attitude of complete indifference to the moral implications of what he was saying, and was quite willing to supply every detail asked about his work:

Counsel: 'And then the railway transports arrived. During what period did these transports arrive and about how many people, roughly, were in a transport?'

Hoess: 'During the whole period up until 1944, certain operations were carried out at irregular intervals in the different countries, so that one cannot speak of a continuous flow of incoming transports. Each series of shipments lasted four to six weeks. During those four to six weeks, two or three trains, containing about two thousand persons each, arrived daily.'

Counsel: 'During an interrogation I had with you the other day you told me that about sixty men were designated to receive these transports, and that these sixty persons too had been bound to the same secrecy described before. Do you still maintain

PLAN OF BIRKENAU CAMP

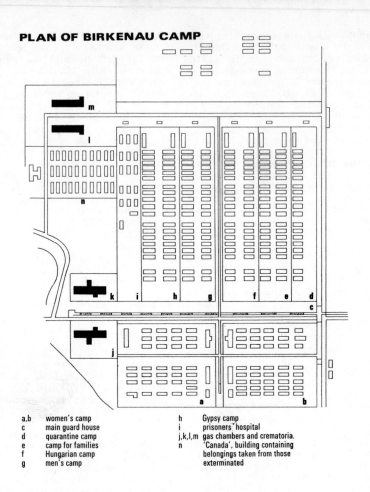

a,b   women's camp
c   main guard house
d   quarantine camp
e   camp for families
f   Hungarian camp
g   men's camp

h   Gypsy camp
i   prisoners' hospital
j,k,l,m   gas chambers and crematoria.
n   'Canada', building containing
      belongings taken from those
      exterminated

that today?'

Hoess: 'Yes, these sixty men were always on hand to take the detainees not capable of work to these provisional installations and, later on, to other ones. This group, consisting of about ten leaders and sub-leaders, as well as doctors and medical personnel, had repeatedly been told both in writing and verbally that they were bound to strictest secrecy as to all that went on in the camps.'

Counsel: 'And after the arrival of the transports did the victims have to dispose of everything they had? Did they have to undress completely; did they have to surrender their valuables? Is this true?'

Hoess: 'Yes.'

Counsel: 'And then they immediately went to their death?'

Hoess: 'Yes.'

Counsel: 'I ask you, according to your knowledge, did these people know what was in store for them?'

Hoess: 'The majority of them did not, for steps were taken to keep them in doubt about it so that suspicion would not arise that they were to go to their death. For instance, all doors and all walls bore inscriptions to the effect that they were going to undergo a delousing operation or take a shower.'

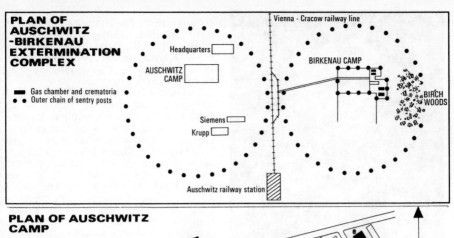

PLAN OF AUSCHWITZ-BIRKENAU EXTERMINATION COMPLEX

Vienna - Cracow railway line

Headquarters

AUSCHWITZ CAMP

■ Gas chamber and crematoria
• • Outer chain of sentry posts

Siemens

Krupp

BIRKENAU CAMP

BIRCH WOODS

Auschwitz railway station

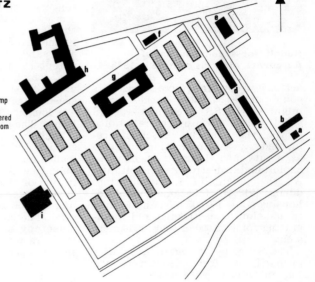

PLAN OF AUSCHWITZ CAMP

▨ living quarters
a house of camp commandant
b main guard house
c commandant's office
d administration of the camp
e crematorium 1
f guard house at the entrance gate to camp
g camp kitchen
h building where newcomers were registered
i building containing belongings taken from those exterminated

Counsel: 'You also told me that even before death definitely set in the victims fell into a state of unconsciousness?'

Hoess: 'Yes. From what I was able to find out myself or from what was told me by medical officers, the time necessary for the arrival of unconsciousness or death varied according to the temperature and the number of people present in the chambers. Loss of consciousness took place after a few seconds or minutes.

Counsel: 'Did you yourself ever sympathise with the victims, thinking of your own family and children?'

Hoess: 'Yes.

Counsel: 'How was it possible, then, for you to carry out these actions?

Hoess: 'In spite of all the doubts which I had, the only one and decisive argument was the strict order and the reason given for it by the Reichsführer Himmler.

What Hoess constructed for the SS was a virtually impregnable community of death. This was scarcely true of the other genocide camps. The story of Treblinka is proof of this; in spite of its sham railway station, built to deceive incoming prisoners that it was some kind of residential labour centre to which they had been brought, resolute

115

Rudolf Hoess, commandant of Auschwitz, after his capture in 1945

action by a combined force of prisoners could indeed frustrate the armed might of the SS. Treblinka was, in effect, closed down by the resistance of its prisoners. But Auschwitz remained, a vast institution as large as a city and designed at once to exploit and to destroy its inhabitants. At the height of its occupation, during 1943–44, it became capable of housing some 100,000 men and women in addition to destroying and incinerating some 12,000 or more prisoners a day.

The SS came to regard Auschwitz primarily as a form of industry, with human beings as its waste product. Despoilation began at the moment of entry into the camp. It is not easy for those who did not endure it to imagine the torture the prolonged period of transportation involved; for several days and nights prisoners could be wedged tightly together in sealed box-wagons with no food, water or sanitation except what they carried themselves. The transportations had a low priority on the railways, and were frequently shunted into sidings where it might be possible to shout to passers-by and barter valuables in return for cans of water, provided the wagon had a ventilation grill large enough for the purpose. The elderly or the sick might well die on the journey and still remain pres-sed up among the living; some people went off their heads, or reverted to forms of primitive desperation in their efforts to survive. The lucky ones were those whose journey was comparatively short.

The main line between Cracow and Vienna passed directly through the heart of the camp complex, though little was to be seen as the express trains sped through what appeared to be a huge barracks, with larger installations kept at some distance from the line. Certain of these, shielded by trees, might be seen a mile and a half away, giving off trails of black smoke from tall chimneys. Only those passengers 'privileged' to know the secrets of genocide would realise that this smoke came from the patent incinerators designed for the SS by Topf and Son of Wiesbaden. (The patent for this fast-burning apparatus, which most ingeniously made use of the body-fat of the corpses to speed the process of their destruction, was lodged after the war at Somerset House. The patent is still pending.)

Each transport was shunted into a siding, and the prisoners were unloaded onto ramps out of sight of the main line. As a prisoner has recorded in one of the many books survivors have written about their experiences: 'Heavy footsteps crunched on the sand. The shout of orders broke the monotony of the wait. The seals of the cars were broken. The door slid slowly open and we could already hear them giving us orders.'

As they half-staggered, half-fell out of the dark wagons into the daylight, the prisoners could feel only sheer physical relief at leaving their nauseating confinement. They were received by a mixed unit of SS officers and guards, supplemented by prisoner helpers. They would be either mocked or bullied by the SS according to the mood of the moment. Sometimes music would be provided by the prisoners' orchestra – tangos and jazz numbers were specially popular to lull the anxieties of the new arrivals. All that mattered to the SS was that they should be immediately cowed into submission, and that those about to be selected for immediate death should not think worse was to happen to them than a visit to the camp bath-house. In any case, most of them were too frightened, dazed, and shamed at their filthy condition to offer any form of resistance – they came from every class and station in life, the Jewish professional classes, intellectuals, business men, artisans and tradesmen, farmers and peasants, all dispossessed, many clinging to their last valuabies, share certificates and bankbooks, jewellery and fur coats, their belongings crushed into handbags, or into suitcases on which they may have tried to squat during the agonies of the journey.

With blows and cuffs from the SS, they would be hastily lined up for inspection by the SS doctors. At Auschwitz the elegant Dr Mengele was notorious for the sadistic pleasure he took in speedily indicating with flicks of his riding whip whether a man or woman was to be preserved for work or die. Each transport was dealt with as summarily as possible; there might well be another on its way in. Any prisoner's hasty attempts to assess what kind of a place he had come to were not likely to tell him much. Auschwitz-Birkenau was a dual camp of such immense size that the electrified barbed-wire fencing round Birkenau alone (the extermination centre) extended for about eight miles; each individual camp, one on each side of the railway, occupied some four square miles. Auschwitz, the industrial centre, was linked up with the special plants constructed by such firms as Siemens, Krupp, and Farben. Watchtowers were constructed at intervals along the electrified fencing; these towers were manned by armed guards of the SS and Waffen-SS, and searchlights could be played over the camp compounds at night.

The gas-chambers and crematoria awaited those who remained unselected for work. The rejects were the elderly, the infirm, the crippled, those showing any sign of mental disturbance, pregnant women, and all women with children up to fourteen or so years of age. Women with children were held by the SS to be pecularily dangerous – they could fight with hysterical energy once they thought their children were being threatened, and they could only too easily create

scenes which developed into mass-disturbance among the other prisoners. It was for this reason that mixed groups of prisoners were often received with a kind of mock paternalism, so that these potential causes of disturbance in the camp could be removed as soon as possible. On the other hand, recalcitrant individuals could always be quietly removed out of sight of the rest and silenced with a shot.

If families were broken up, which was normally the case, they were merely told that they would be reunited after bathing. The able-bodied men and women were marched off to be stripped, numbered by tattoo, and clad in unclean prison garb. Their shelter in future would be the over-crowded wooden barracks. The prisoners due to die were taken off to the distant gas-chambers in service trucks.

The ante-rooms to the gas-chambers were, as Hoess pointed out at the trial, disguised as bath-houses. Anxiety that they might be something worse was allayed by members of the SS supervising staff being present while the prisoners stripped. Controlled by the SS, special gangs *(Sonderkommandos)* made up of prisoners trusted up to a point, and well bribed, undertook the final, repulsive task of extermination. Shifts of about one hundred men worked in each of the four gas-chambers and crematoria. The naked prisoners were led from the undressing-hall into the gas-chamber for what they still believed, or were intended to believe, was bathing. Sometimes music was piped through over loudspeakers. When all were safely in, the staff silently withdrew, and the prisoners were sealed up. Meanwhile, vans falsely marked with the insignia of the Red Cross had brought up supplies of the Zyclon B crystals from which the gas was created for injection through vents in the roof into the gas-chamber.

After an interval of twenty minutes or so, the fumes from the poison gas were extracted by patent mechanical ventilators, and the prisoner commando moved in, wearing gas-masks and protective clothing, and carrying hose-pipes. They had to become as

Above: Prisoners arrive at Auschwitz
Right: Crematoria at Sachsenhausen

oblivious as possible to the sight which inevitably met them – the great mound of bodies reflecting in their postures the last, desperate struggle for air as those who still survived climbed up over the bodies of the dead and dying in order to gasp in the last, thin remnants of clean air. The Sonderkommando hosed the stained corpses, dragging them apart and then loading them for the descent by elevator to the crematoria below. Here the last desecration took place – gold teeth were wrenched out from the dead jaws with pliers and thrown into baths of acid, and valuable hair was shaved from the heads of the women. The corpses were now valueless. Automatically they were fed in batches of three into one of the fifteen ovens which made up the normal installation in each of the crematoria. The destructive capacity of one crematorium was forty-five bodies every twenty minutes. The problem in the extermination camps was never that of killing people, it was the disposal of their bodies. Mass-burial in great trenches, the original method before the installation of the patented crematoria, was as unsafe as it was unhygienic, and it always left the SS with the uneasy feeling that their secret work of destruction might well catch up with them. Hoess was immensely relieved when the crematoria proved so efficient.

Nevertheless, the SS became utterly dependent on the use of prisoner-labour for these mass-exterminations. The kind of men employed were those who cynically accepted that it was better to have a comparatively good time doing this work and 'living it up' while they were off duty, than to work in the factories as slaves on a diet which was worse than chronic starvation. The SS accepted the situation realistically and were prepared to let these men eat and drink their fill, and even live in comparative luxury. Their normal allotment of life on this level was four months; then they were themselves shot and

cremated with the rest.

The community of staff and prisoners at Auschwitz-Birkenau soon sorted itself out, as human beings will, into a complex hierarchy of privilege. At the very top was Hoess himself, wearing the finest uniform but only on rare occasions to be seen, surrounded by his staff, within the working areas of the camp. He lived with his wife in the Commandant's house nearby; his wife got what social life she could by associating with other SS officer's wives from the married quarters. She loved clothes, and she was dressed by a Jewess from Prague, skilled in haute couture, who had a team of twelve seamstresses from the camp at her disposal. Under Hoess came the senior SS staff, men who declined in 'quality' as Hitler's demands for Nordic manpower on the battlefronts denuded the SS of both officers and men. Hoess was left for the most part with the riff-raff and the scourings of foreign recruits to the SS and the Waffen-SS, who undertook perimeter guard-duty and often spoke no German.

It has to be remembered that although Himmler's office staff and the men in charge of the camps were technically exempt from actual military service, which meant by 1942–43 the rigours of the Eastern Front, the active 'elite' were increasingly called upon to take to the field of battle when Hitler's devouring militarism led to pressurised recruitment of every able-bodied German. Himmler, therefore, was to be left with a hard core of traditional SS men in the older age-groups and an ever-increasing number of 'foreigners', who were drafted, often very willingly, to serve him as supplementary police, camp guards, petty administrative staff in the camps, and the like. In the end, the concentration camps were to be made as far as possible self-operative by the increasing use of prisoner-staff supervised by a comparatively small SS ground staff who were in turn supervised by a handful of the old 'elite', the camp commandant and his aides.

Although up to 40,000 SS men and women were technically in charge of

The orchestra at Auschwitz

the total concentration-camp system inside and outside Germany, with its hundreds of subsidiaries in the form of minor labour camps and units spread far and wide wherever they were wanted, the old dream of an SS elite force was by now in a sorry state. No one would think of Hoess of Auschwitz, Kramer of Belsen, or Koch and his wife Ilse at Buchenwald as setting such high standards; far less had the SS ranks in the camps any pretensions left of being 'model' Germans. Some of them are being put on trial in Germany even now, old men for the most part of poor mentality and brutal demeanour – many of them, in the 1940s, police or army rejects without the capacity or inclination for skilled work, some declining into petty criminals who saw in camp service the opportunity for graft and the exercise of power. Some were real sadists, such as Wilhelm Boger, the flogger, who was among those put on trial in Frankfurt during 1964. Boger had been a career policeman before joining the SS in 1932. Most, however, were insensitive and brutalised morons of a kind any nation can produce if the streets, prisons, and brothels are scoured. The best men of Germany were on the fighting fronts, or doing skilled work in the factories. The worst gravitated towards the concentration camps, or into the guard rooms and interrogation cells of the Gestapo.

It was obvious that to organise, maintain, and discipline a community of anything between 50,000 and 100,000 workers, the SS would have to use prisoner-staff. This at once led to a complex hierarchy created by the prisoners themselves, among whom, it must be remembered, were many men and women of the highest qualifications and ability from every walk of life and from many different countries. By no means all were Jews. The camps became increasingly cosmopolitan, where the survival of the fittest often meant the survival of the most astute, or the most corrupt, as well as of those honest men and women with a high capacity for self-control and planned endurance. Thus the very worst and the very best survived alongside each other and assumed positions of minor authority in the camps. In Auschwitz this hierarchy amounted at any one time to several thousand.

Each prisoner wore a special badge which picked him out at sight for what he was. The basic insignia were a green triangle for convicted criminals, a purple triangle for Jehovah's Witnesses (who were dedicated pacifists), a red triangle for political prisoners, a pink triangle for homosexuals, and a black triangle for 'anti-socials', that is, prisoners who were held to be shiftless or unemployable, which included the Gypsies. All Jews wore an additional, yellow triangle superimposed upside down, their combined insignia forming the double-triangle of the six-point Star of David.

The criminal class provided many of the key prisoner-supervisors – the so-called Kapos. They frequently acted with brutality to their fellow prisoners and used their superior status alike to curry favour with the SS and exact privileges from their helpless victims. They got more food, more graft, more sex, and slightly better living conditions. The Kapos became the most notorious of the SS's collaborators in the exploitation of the captives; they undertook, often with some relish, the dirty work of camp discipline and the passing-on of unwelcome orders. Since an SS man did not normally address an ordinary prisoner if he could help it – the prisoners, faced by an SS man or woman, had to stand, cap in hand, three paces away, and never speak unless required to – it was the Kapos who passed on the routine orders. But over and above the Kapos, prisoners were needed to undertake a host of menial administrative and 'domestic' tasks – to act as secretaries, interpreters, clerks, domestic helps in the SS married quarters, gardeners, and workers, skilled and unskilled, in the camp hospitals and kitchens. Foreign workers who spoke German had an immediate advantage over those who could not. Best treated of all, perhaps, were the prisoner-doctors, both Jewish and non-Jewish. Their skills were in perpetual demand.

For all prisoners whose aim was to survive, it was necessary to use their wits to work their way through to some camp job for the SS which offered them protective covering. Any weakness in a prisoner was soon discovered. If he gave way to despair, there was ample opportunity for suicide, either by getting himself shot, beaten to death, or killing himself by clinging to the electrified fencing. If his health gave, there was little hope for him. If the prisoner were a woman and became pregnant, a quick abortion was essential – for women discovered to be pregnant went automatically to the gas-chamber. The prisoners' philosophy of survival worked in phases of three months. If you despaired you would be finished inside three months; if you showed signs of knowing how to look after yourself, you might well survive through your second three months; if you managed to survive for nine months, you might well survive altogether because you must by then have shown yourself too useful to destroy. The thing was, never to put a foot wrong with your superiors – SS or Kapo – and to reveal some talent or skill which was needed at the right place and the right time to become a privileged prisoner. Naturally you avoided the worse forms of prison labour – being assigned to the latrine-cleaning or the corpse-carrying gangs. The most hideous tasks in the camp, that of the *Sonderkommandos* in charge of the gas-chambers and crematoria, ranked as the most highly privileged, but it was a short life.

One woman prisoner has estimated that in 1943, some 32,000 women were confined in Birkenau. Of these some 7,000 might at any one time be ill, probably in hospital, but considered 'orth curing for further work, unless the pressure of incoming prisoners was very great. Some 400 to 500 would carry some form of privilege, acting as hut seniors, for example, in charge of the barrack-rooms, and so forth up to being a recognised prisoner-doctor, a very senior grade for a prisoner and exempting him or her from most of the severer disciplinary routines, such as roll-call. Apart from these privileged jobs around the camps, often

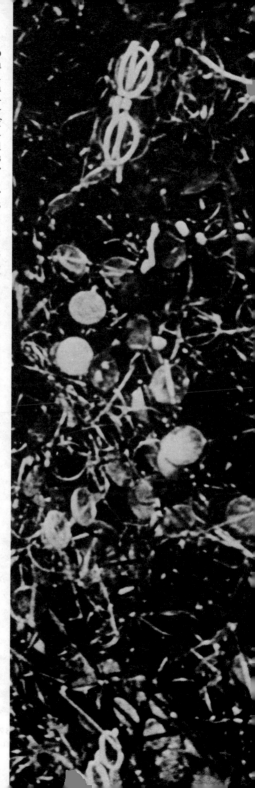

Spectacles taken from gassed prisoners

Above: What kind of man became a guard? Two SS men examine a gold bracelet.
Right: Two 'Kapos' drag away a fellow prisoner – with tongs

bringing relative freedom of movement around the compounds, both men and women were subject to appalling labour conditions. They had to parade in the open twice daily, whatever the weather, for roll-call – the first assembly beginning not later than 5 am in the summer and at 6 am in the winter. They were counted by their Kapos, and any dead had to be laid out alongside the ranks of the living, who stood to attention waiting. The dead and the living alike were numbers and had to be checked out as such by the SS, who normally came on duty around 7 am. Discipline was maintained by the Kapos and the SS themselves by the free use of whips and truncheons or with blows direct from the fist. Liquid food, such as survived transport in soup-barrels from the kitchens, followed the roll-call. Roving prisoners might attack those detailed for carrying the heavy barrels in order to filch some extra mouthfuls of soup at the other prisoners' expense.

The prisoners then moved out to their daily work, sometimes accompanied by music. Prisoner-musicians,

A roll-call at Mauthausen. The prisoners were often forced to stand on their feet, naked, while waiting for the SS

Prisoners with the necessary skill were even permitted on occasion to mount a cabaret show, at which the SS might well be represented in the audience. For the prisoners, these crumbs of comfort, ghosts of culture or of entertainment from a world fast becoming remote and faded, were precious and life-giving. Proficiency in sport or show-business might well lead to an extra allowance of food. A further curiosity of the concentration camps was the occasional 'shops' for arts and crafts; prisoners with the necessary skills were employed making objets d'art for senior officers in the SS.

For prisoners who refused to despair and who entered upon the 'underground' life open to 'successful' prisoners in the camps, certain things became possible. If their bodies were sufficiently nourished they might take part in sport – football or boxing, for example, or a treasured visit to the camp brothel (confined to 'Aryans') where the girls were prisoners seeking survival and privilege in a particular form open to them. They received small gifts of money or presents filched from the great quantity of goods arriving with the incoming prisoners. The SS were, after all, men of the world and winked at slight exchanges of this kind, since it kept their 'Aryan' prisoner-staff in better heart. Lower ranks even patronised the brothel themselves, seeing that the girls were Nordic.

like prisoner-doctors had their unique uses. In any case, it kept them alive a little longer, and did no active harm. The Nazi pursuit of culture did not stop at this. Prisoners were made to sing as they marched to their work, or as they stood on parade in the cold and the rain, or under the hot sun, perhaps stripped naked for punishment or as a result of some sadistic whim. On Sunday afternoons, when all work stopped, concerts of classical music might be given in the camp compounds. Auschwitz boasted an orchestra as well as a jazz-band.

What was never winked at was any theft discovered in the great sorting-house known as 'Canada'. It was here that everything of real value came for checking, packing, and delivery to Germany in the same wagons (duly cleaned out) that had brought the prisoners to the camp. This formed part of SS business enterprise. Pohl reported that in February 1943 781 wagon-loads had left the camp for Germany. 245 of these were filled with clothing and one van contained three tons of women's hair. The gold extracted from teeth was sent away in the form of ingots and deposited in the *Reichsbank*, credited to the SS.

Warsaw ghetto. *Above:* SD men confront Rabbis. *Right:* Jews are given a loaf of bread on their way to Treblinka

In the black-market of the camps, prisoners existing on the lowest level would barter rags to patch or supplement their prison clothing; those on a higher level acquired whatever they could get away with to add dignity or distinction to their appearance. Prisoners who had reached the 'heights' – senior block prisoners, or the highest of all, the senior camp prisoner, or *Lägerälteste*, men and women who even had their own servants or recognised assistants – could, provided they did not flout the SS, turn regulation wear into the most expensively 'fashionable' attire. The camp became like some strange parody of an ill-conceived English public school in the 19th century –

with prefects lording it over their juniors and exacting every kind of base privilege in exchange for their 'patronage', while at the same time they curried favour with the 'masters' on whom their petty powers depended.

This kind of 'caste' uniform among the men turned the shapeless prison cap into a trim affair with a smart peak, the dirty prison coat, like a pyjama top, into an elegantly cut jacket of excellent material with 'fancy' pockets, while possession of a well-laundered pullover was the sign of ultimate privilege in a society abject with filth. High boots worn instead of the ill-fitting clogs, characteristic of the under-privileged and smart breeches or trousers with a sharp crease, showed a prisoner had a tailor or launderer at his service among the lesser prisoners. He bought the goods, material, and the service

General Jürgen Stroop (peaked cap) in charge of razing the Warsaw ghetto

itself at high rates on the camp's black market. For women smartness took the form of silk stockings, a well-cut skirt, a high-necked sweater, and a plain silk head-scarf. The high boot, well-polished by a prisoner-servant, was obligatory for a prisoner of distinction of either sex. The SS took all this in good part, making the obvious, school-masterly jokes at the 'privileged' prisoner's expense – 'Hello Isaac, still alive!'

Yet to be caught stealing from the rich resources of 'Canada' was to be stripped, flattened on a block, and beaten. The more daring among the prisoners, men or girls, who had the dangerous privilege of working in 'Canada', still managed to smuggle out a considerable amount. Hardened prisoners learned to survive the beatings, as they learned to survive standing naked in the heat or the cold. For most, the worst punishment of all was the stark hunger, a continual gnawing ache in the stomach, and more utterly demoralising than any other, with the exception of continuous torture. So crusts of bread, however stale, were basic currency in

the black market among the prisoners. Self-control broke down most easily following seemingly trivial losses in food through error or theft. It was for this reason that the greatest privilege of all was one which brought with it a scrap extra in rations. Second only to food was the privilege of cleanliness. It might seem worth working in direct daily contact with the SS as a servant or seamstress, for example, if, as a result, soap or water were allowed. Starvation and lack of hygiene were the primary causes of chronic sickness in the camp, along with the impure water, which had to be boiled for the SS – but not, of course, for the prisoners.

The community of Auschwitz, therefore, was one in which the vices of the outside world became exaggerated and grotesque. Few were free from one form or another of corruption, while over all lay the blanket of despair. For those with access to alcohol, SS and prisoners alike, inebriation brought relief. Sexual promiscuity was rampant among those few sufficiently well-fed to feel the need for sex. Sickness, like pregnancy, was

The Warsaw rising. *Left:* Jewish fighters are led away to be shot. *Above:* German soldier in action

a thing to be hidden in a community where both were occupational hazards. Gradually the captors and survivors among the captive began to acquire a *modus vivendi*, a perverted institutional sense which led to a code of acceptance, a live-and-let-live weariness with the whole ugly business, especially when the war was ceasing to go well for the Germans, and the lower grade of SS man was no longer interested in maintaining his 'elite' mask. A camp 'psychology' developed, a curious inverted cameraderie; the SS would joke with their favourites, and predatory love affairs developed in certain quarters. Even Hoess for a while indulged himself in a mistress, a Jewish prisoner from Vienna.

Underneath the camp 'atmosphere', a resistance movement eventually formed which took advantage of every weakness or corruption in the SS and established a network of espionage. Resistance mostly took the form of surreptitious sabotage and

various kinds of 'hold' over the more susceptible of the SS staff. Secret radio receivers were maintained for news, and it was even possible on occasion to broadcast information to the Polish resistance outside. Acts of sabotage had to avoid inviting SS reprisal, which it was only too easy to excite; the main concern was to preserve life by tampering with names listed for extermination. Escapes were not encouraged because of the severity of the penalties exacted. Escapes nevertheless took place, but in the vast majority of cases these prisoners were either recaptured or shot – or both, their bodies exposed as a warning in the compounds.

The camp inmates involved in resistance were astonishingly well-informed about the progress of the war. When the mid-war years saw the tide begin to turn against the Nazis, and Russian retaliation on the Eastern Front was an acknowledged fact, a measure of hope spread among

133

the 'survivors' in the camp, which was, after all in the path of the Russian armies.

Rudolf Vrba, a young Slovakian Jewish prisoner in Auschwitz from 1942 to 1944, noticed preparations were being made early in 1944 to extend the railway siding which served the camp so that the line would lead directly to the extermination plant. With Fred Wetzler, a friend from the same town in Slovakia, he determined to escape in order to bring warnings outside that it seemed the genocide operations were to be stepped up. The preparations were, in fact, for the extermination of the great numbers of Hungarian Jews who had hitherto remained untouched. Vrba and Wetzler did in fact escape in April 1944, just in advance of the holocaust of the Hungarian Jews at Auschwitz, which lasted throughout the spring and summer of 1944.

Vrba's warnings, and the detailed statistics and information he and Wetzler were able to provide, had little effect, though their report (a document of some 20,000 words, with maps and diagrams) was sent in secret to the Jewish Council in Budapest, and later in translation reached Churchill, Roosevelt, and the Pope. Yet nothing was done, and the Hungarian Jews were transported to their deaths. Not even the essential railway line, the approaches to Auschwitz, were bombed, let alone the crematoria. Eichmann had arrived in Budapest the previous March with a team of SS deportation experts. His arrival symbolised German ascendency in Hungary with the connivance of Admiral Horthy, the Regent, and it would seem that the Jewish representatives with whom he had to deal were prepared to comply with Eichmann's desire to deport the Jews to the 'labour' camps (as they were described) in the north. Eichmann was ready in April to negotiate the sale of certain Jewish liberties, arranging for the transfer of some 1,600 prominent Jews and their families to Switzerland for $1,000 a head. The Jewish leaders in Hungary put Vrba's warnings aside rather than imperil these private negotiations, or so it would seem; whatever the reason, they let their fellows be sent without

protest to what they must have realised would be their destruction in Auschwitz. Eichmann's transports began to roll during late April and early May.

The very respectable members of the local Jewish councils who represented their fellows in the communities overrun by the Germans took, in general, the line of least resistance. They were made up of rabbis, professors, lawyers, professional men, and others of the pacific middle-class. At the best they tried as far as possible to ease the difficult position, and few of them believed at first that genocide, as distinct from more traditional forms of persecution, were to be practised against them. The SS agents, naturally enough, spoke only of deployment for labour in the east. At the worst, some of the Jewish councils might be said to have betrayed their racial kindred, or acted in over-blind compliance with whatever the Germans demanded. It was the Jewish councils which did much of Eichmann's work for him – they compiled the names and addresses of all Jews in their community, listed whatever the community owned in property and goods, and provided all other details and statistics required of them. It was they, too, who summoned the Jews together on the day of departure, spoke to them, comforted them, kept them quiet and obedient. And as a reward they themselves were often allowed to remain a little longer in peace, isolated in their households until they too were swept up with their families and transported to death or slave-labour.

Yet here and there pockets of resistance grew up among the victims, as had happened at Treblinka. The most heroic and most celebrated of all is the uprising in the Warsaw Ghetto. The Ghetto itself, as we have seen, had been used as a source of slave-labour until, in 1942, its population of some 400,000 Jews was reduced to 60,000 following transportations to the extermination camps, primarily Treblinka, sixty miles away. Early in 1943 Himmler had been shocked to discover that much of the remaining Jewish labour in the Ghetto was being exploited by SS

The resistance of the 56,000 Jews left in the ghetto astonished Stroop

agents in a private black market of their own instead of being employed in armaments manufacture. He ordered the final evacuation of the Ghetto, but before his orders could be carried out Jewish partisans, who had a secret cache of arms, began their revolt against the SS. They held out for thirty-three days against SS-General Stroop's armoured units, which totalled 2,000 men. These, typically enough by now, consisted not of Germans, but of Poles and Lithuanians, supplemented by two training battalions of the Waffen-SS. Stroop eventually either killed or arrested for extermination every Jew left in the place; then he burned the Ghetto to the ground. Afterwards, he sent Himmler a handsomely bound report, illustrated by photographs, and entitled, *The Warsaw Ghetto Is No More.* Warsaw provided the SS with a salutary reminder that the Jews in the mass must be handled with diplomatic circumspection until they were finally locked up in the transport wagons and sent on their way to Auschwitz.

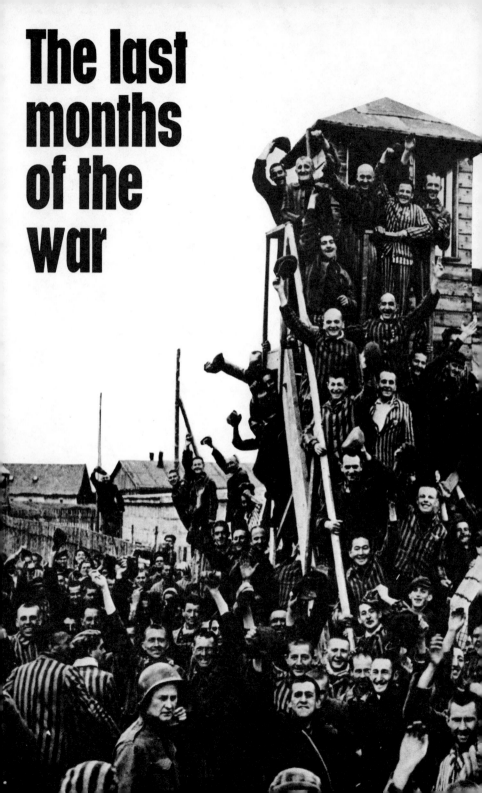

The last months of the war

The massacre of the Hungarian Jews was the last act of mass extermination to be undertaken at Auschwitz. By the end of 1944, the genocide camps were threatened by the advance of Soviet forces. Himmler and the SS were having second thoughts about the whole extermination programme, and the growing problem which the camps represented, with the great horde of prisoners who were becoming less and less useful as labour and more and more difficult to dispose of in such numbers as dead bodies. The SS exploitation market was fading. Himmler was under constant pressure in private by both Schellenberg of the SD and Kersten, his masseur, to ease the position of the Jews and even to release them, while on an official level he was being urged by the International Red Cross to permit their officers to visit the camps and arrange for the alleviation of suffering and the supply of Red Cross food

and parcels. He was, in fact, in a state of neurotic indecision as to the best thing to do. His obstinate uncertainty was to last until the final days of the war.

On 20th July 1944 the attempt made on Hitler's life by members of the resistance mainly in the German army had been all-but successful, and the SS had been responsible for the immediate, on-the-spot investigations at Hitler's headquarters at Rastenburg, where the time-bomb which so nearly killed him had been placed. It had soon become apparent that a conspiracy of some considerable size had existed within the army to dispose of Hitler by *coup d'état* and set up a new government to negotiate peace with the Allies. Himmler was deeply disturbed not only by this, but by his certainty that Hitler himself was on the way to suffering a mental breakdown. Meanwhile, one of his personal ambitions

had at least come true – Hitler had created him Commander-in-Chief of the Reserve Army, based in Germany, on the very day of the failure of the assassination attempt.

The mid-winter of 1944–45 saw the tragi-comic climax of Himmler's extraordinary career. He was now not only *Reichsführer SS* and Minister of the Interior, but in command of one of Hitler's armies; in December 1944 he was put in charge of Army Group Rhine. He also assumed direct command of the Waffen-SS.

He set about fulfilling his new duties with all the sincere, egocentric stupidity of the born amateur. His experience on the battlefield was nil; his army training was solely that of an officer cadet who had been little more than a schoolboy at the time.

Below: Hitler and Mussolini after the bomb plot. *Right:* Minister of the Interior with SS apprentices

Having failed disastrously during his few weeks in the west, Himmler, surrounded by an equally inexperienced staff of SS men, was sent in January 1945 to try his luck against the Russians, who had by now overrun East Prussia and were threatening the whole of northern Germany. Here once again his grasp of affairs was demonstrably hopeless, and he finally retired to his favourite nursing-home at Hohenleichen, issuing useless orders from his bed. Finally, in February 1945, General Guderian managed to force Hitler to release Himmler from any further activities connected with the army.

Himmler spent the last months of the war wavering between thoughts of trying to negotiate a separate peace with the Allies and deciding how best to get himself and the SS out of the hopeless chaos into which the whole concentration camp system had fallen. The great processions of

prisoners from the east had been painfully and cruelly evacuated on foot during the months following September 1944. When the Russians entered Auschwitz in January 1945, they found only 3,000 helpless invalids left in the camp buildings. The position in the remaining hundred or so concentration camps early in 1945 is difficult to determine. One survey in mid-January 1945 gives the numbers of men and women prisoners in the concentration camps in Germany as 714,211, of which 202,674 were women; about one-third of these prisoners were Jewish. The number of SS guards was given as 40,000. But many prisoners – perhaps a quarter of a million – were to die during the forced marches in this final winter of the war. Extermination, therefore, did not stop at the crematoria.

During the last weeks, during March and April, Himmler gradually came to accept the necessity of releasing numbers of Jewish prisoners for evacuation to neutral Switzerland and to Scandinavia under the aegis of the Red Cross, while camps such as Belsen, hopelessly overloaded beyond its 8,000 capacity became a natural death-camp in which no one from the commandant, Kramer, downwards could do much more than watch the prisoners die. Himmler finally yielded the camp to the British on 10th April. The first British investigator, Captain Derrick Sington, entered the camp five days later and came face-to-face with SS-Captain Kramer, the first of the fully-experienced SS camp commandants formally to meet a British officer.

It was during April 1945 that the British and American armies learned at first hand some part of the SS extermination policy. Captured SS and Gestapo records were soon to bring to light those crimes which could not be seen.

Belsen

Above: Kramer, Commandant of Belsen
Left: SS guards are forced to load the bodies of their victims on to trucks for transportation to mass graves, watched by schoolchildren. The full extent of SS savagery was only revealed when the Allies liberated the camps.
Below: General view of Belsen

Aftermath: the displaced peoples

In a world war in which the esti-mated total loss of life reached some fifty-five million men, women, and children, the SS must have accounted for not less than one fifth. Not all the losses during the war years can be accurately calculated. However, the worst losses were those sustained in eastern Europe: the Russians claimed to have lost an estimated 13,000,000 in the armed forces, of whom some three and a half million died while in captivity, many of them through extermination, while some seven mil-lion civilians died 'through occupa-tion and deportation' (Stalin's words). The Germans took 5,754,000 prisoners of war from the Soviet Union, about two-thirds of these during the first seven months of the invasion. The Poles lost some six million dead, well over five million as a result of German action after the fall of Poland. Over 300,000 Czechs were sent to con-centration camps; of these only some 75,000 survived. In all, Czechoslovakia lost 360,000 people through execu-tions, shooting, and death in the camps.

As against this, the Germans them-selves lost nearly three million dead in the armed forces, and an equal number of civilians – half of these, it is important to to remember, as a result of the violently enforced depor-tations from the east after the war, a form of vengeance on those alien occupants brought in by Himmler during 1940–41. A comparatively small force within the SS – mainly 3,000 men in the Action Groups, some 40,000 men and women responsible in one way or another for the organisation and maintenance of the concentration camps, together with the killers in the security police forces of the SS and the Gestapo both inside and out-side Germany – were continuously engaged in the pursuit and extermi-nation of 'unwanted' peoples and those considered to offer some threat to Hitler's Reich. Within five years, Himmler's forces substantially af-fected the distribution and balance of population in many parts of eastern Europe, and they destroyed over five million of the 8.3 million Jews remain-

German refugees cling to the train bringing them from the east in 1945

A column of peasants with their belongings flee from the Russians. Many would remain homeless for years

ing in those parts of Europe Germany occupied after 1939.

The burden of suffering imposed on Europe by the SS did not end with the extermination of so many millions in the death camps. Once the war was over, the mass movements of displaced people both away from and back into Germany began; a large proportion of this uprooting of men, women, and children was the result of the original 'exchange' of populations organised by the SS during the first year of the war. The slave-workers acquired from the east began the trek back to ther native lands, in only too many cases merely to find their homes and properties either destroyed or occupied by hostile strangers; on the other hand, the massacre and expulsion of more-or-less innocent German civilians by the liberated peoples of eastern Europe led to some ten million unwanted Germans pouring into the four Zones of Germany between May and October 1945, mostly from Poland and Czechoslovakia. These wanderers were to be augmented by a further two and a half million who came somewhat later; of the total, West Germany (the Federal Republic, as it was to become) absorbed approaching nine million.

Yet further to this, some four million Germans were to flee from East Germany (the German Democratic Republic) to the West before the construction of the Berlin Wall in 1961. This evacuation, at least, was not the direct result of Himmler's racial obsessions, as were the movements and counter-movements of millions of unhappy, unwanted people

who in 1945 entered a Germany so ill-prepared to receive them – a nation stunned by defeat and without any form of constitutional government. In the British zone alone, the proportion of properties totally destroyed was one in four, with one in two badly damaged; in certain cities which had been the target for saturation bombing by the Allies, these proportions were even higher. Yet in the zone there were initially two million displaced people, most of them former slave workers anxious to be repatriated to the east. In addition, there were the prisoners of war on both sides to be officially 'cleared' and sent home. Fortunately, it was spring; the winter was over and the summer months lay ahead, during which some attempt could be made by the occupying authorities to sort out this human disaster.

Though the first stages of these readjustments of displaced populations were resolved during the first summer of peace, the hard core of those who had literally nowhere to go were settled temporarily in the refugee camps established by the Allies in their zones. By October some seven million prisoners and slave workers out of the eleven million originally forced by the SS to leave their homes had been repatriated with the help of UNRRA (the United Nations Relief and Rehabilitation Agency), though in the course of the ebb and flow in the tide of suffering, many came back again because they found only hostility when they returned to their former homes in the east. They returned, not because they wanted to live in Germany (naturally enough), but because they hoped the Western Allies would be more helpful than the Communist authorities at home, and if possible arrange for their transport to the United States or (if they were Jews) to Palestine.

By June 1945, the British military government had to refuse further entry to refugees in its zone, and the Americans followed suit in April 1947. In 1946–47, the numbers of the displaced stood at some 600,000 (one third of them Jews), waiting helplessly in the refugee camps for some solution to be found for their future. Yet no one wanted them, because the burden of cost in maintaining them (some $9 million a month) fell on the occupying powers, mainly in fact on the United States. Various organisations were set up for their immediate relief and to help promote their migration to the countries willing to receive them. In the end something approaching two and a half millions were either settled abroad or died of illness or old age in the overcrowded camps. The problem was to last until the early 1960s, and a World Refugee Year was organised during 1959–60 to remind us all of the residue of these forgotten people, once victims of the SS, whom nobody wanted and who were still waiting for that most precious of all gifts – an immigration permit to some desired land. The principal receiving areas for the Jewish refugees were the United States and, following the cessation

Above: Concentration camp survivors on their way home. *Below:* The suicide of Himmler, 23rd May, 1945, after giving himself up to the British

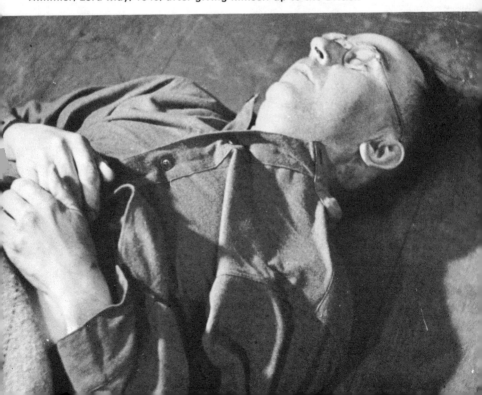

of the British mandate in May 1948, the new state of Israel.

Of the more prominent leaders of the SS, only Kaltenbrunner (Heydrich's successor at RSHA) was in captivity awaiting trial for war crimes. Pohl, Kramer, and Ohlendorf were also under arrest. Eichmann was for a while held in captivity by the Americans, but he posed as a corporal in the Luftwaffe and passed unrecognised. Afraid that his identity might be discovered, he managed to get away, and follow the standard escape route for the more notorious Nazis to Latin America. His abduction by Israeli agents in 1960, and subsequent trial in Jerusalem the following year became one of the most remarkable events of the postwar years. Hoess managed to avoid arrest for almost a year, but was eventually discovered by the British Military Police just in time, as we have seen, to give important evidence at the International Military Tribunal in Nuremberg, which was already in session. Müller, head of the Gestapo, disappeared, probably to Russia, and still remains untraced, the constant subject of rumour. He is now seventy. Himmler had managed to commit suicide on 23rd May, after having admitted his identity to his British captors. His body lies in an unmarked grave near Lüneberg.

Most prominent among the organisations which had for some time been attempting to relieve the sufferings of the prisoners in the concentration camps was the International Red Cross. During the 1920s and 1930s attempts had been made at successive international congresses to obtain agreement covering the protection of deported civilian refugees in time of war, similar to conditions already agreed for the protection of prisoners of war. But no pact covering civilians existed in 1939; the Red Cross had been refused the right to visit the concentration camps, though from 1943 Red Cross parcels were permitted for non-Jewish prisoners. (It can be imagined to what extent the SS guards and the Kapos took their toll of these parcels.) Nevertheless, between November 1943 and May 1945, some 750,000 Red Cross parcels had been sent to the camps. At the same time, the first stages in securing information about the identity of non-Jewish prisoners in SS hands had begun.

During the last months of the war, the Red Cross had managed to achieve some further penetration into the camps, small and sporadic though it was. In January 1945 Red Cross officials had met Richard Glücks in Berlin. They had understood him to be a senior administrator in charge of the camps. Though this and subsequent meetings had proved abortive, individual Red Cross representatives had managed to get glimpses of certain camps during meetings with their commandants. As we have seen, pressure had already been brought to bear on Himmler by Schellenberg and by Kersten, his masseur, which had led to preservation of a certain, limited number of Jewish lives, and from February 1945 Count Bernadotte of the Swedish Red Cross had been in direct touch with Himmler and had managed, with infinite difficulty, to extract some measure of agreement from him to alleviate the lot of Jewish women prisoners and secure for them some limited evacuation from the camps. Red Cross officials had also been allowed to bring lorry loads of supplies into Germany to help starving prisoners taking part in the death marches from the camps which the SS had been forced to evacuate, especially the thousands sent west on foot from Oranienburg. The bodies of men, women, and children lying by the wayside had marked the route of these terrible processions conducted under SS guard and openly revealing the condition in which the SS kept their captives.

This had been only a few weeks before Himmler finally yielded his camps to the Allied forces, and the full record of the SS had become public. The world saw the first Allied newsreels and press photographs of the prisoners staring at their liberators through the wire fencing, bewildered as the thought of relief entered their minds. For many it was too late; they died of disease, starvation or sheer excitement under the horrified eyes of Allied soldiers and doctors.

Arolsen: the Red Cross tracing centre

The first stages in the daunting and seemingly impossible task of re-joining the millions of loose threads which the broken families of central Europe represented in 1945 was assumed by the German Red Cross for German nationals and for the non-Germans by the Central Tracing Bureau placed in 1946 under UNNRA. The Bureau, later renamed the International Tracing Service, eventually became the responsibility of the International Red Cross with its headquarters in a large building in Arolsen, near Kassel in central Germany. Arolsen itself employs a staff of some 240 linguists, legal and archive experts and their assistants and handles questions of individual identity and family information – problems which in 1968 still covered some 12,000 cases a month.

The captured records of the SS and Gestapo, including the records of certain concentration camps themselves (notably Dachau and Buchenwald), were handed over to these various tracing authorities. These records proved to be, in certain cases, astonishingly detailed, and visitors to Arolsen can study the card indices compiled by the SS clerks recording the particulars of the prisoners passing through their hands. There are, of course, vast gaps in these captured records; the SS destroyed what they could when the collapse of Germany was certain by the spring of 1945. But much remained intact and helped the German Red Cross to handle over a quarter of a million appeals during the first twenty years between 1945 and 1965 by parents searching for lost children. Taking the German nationals alone, some 300,000 children were lost or missing, separated from their parents; of these some 127,000 were successfully traced. The German Red Cross also dealt with the repatriation of missing prisoners-of-war and civilians – 1.27 million German soldiers and nearly 200,000 civilians were still listed as missing twenty years after the war.

But this was little compared with the problems that faced those concerned to trace the non-German civilian victims of the war – the dead, the missing, the children stolen by the SS and living now as adopted

Germans under changed names. By 1968 the records at Arolsen exceeded twenty-eight million index cards cross-referencing some seven million individual cases. This represents the true record of the SS, and is largely concerned with Jewish victims. The Red Cross experts have been faced with astonishing tasks of detection owing to the tangle of nationalities involved among the SS clerical staff, who spelt names of prisoners recorded as arriving in the camps, working or dying in a variety of spellings. There are, according to officials at Arolsen, 160 ways of spelling John. The Red Cross Tracing Service has had to deal with some 45,000 cases of people called Schwartz, and yet there are forty-four ways of spelling this name. On the other hand, the German SS clerks, faced with especially difficult Slav names, merely spelled them phonetically. The SS clerks, whether German or non-German, were often barely literate, and spelled the names of prisoners carelessly, often changing the spelling as the prisoner passed from hand to hand.

The enquiries dealt with at Arolsen vary widely. Many have been concerned with re-uniting relatives separated while passing through the labour camps. A typical case is that of a Jewish family of husband, wife, and son who had been sent together to Auschwitz. The wife had been exterminated on arrival, and the father transferred to work at Buchenwald; the son was retained at Auschwitz. After the war, father and son as entirely separate refugees, had both been sent to Israel. The son, in his late teens and held to be an orphan, had asked to be sent to the United States during the same period as his father had been trying to trace him through Arolsen. They were finally united just before the boy was due to leave for America. More complex, perhaps, has been the work of uniting surviving parents with children whom the SS had placed in foster homes to be brought up as German nationals. The British film, *The Divided Heart* (1954), was based on a true story of particular poignancy, in which a ten-year-old boy, devoted to his kindly German foster-parents, had to be restored to his Yugoslav

mother, who had been traced by officials of the International Refugee Organisation, the predecessors in this work of the International Red Cross. The boy, of course, knew no Serbo-Croat, and his mother no German. There were only too many cases of this kind, which had to be handled with every measure of tact and humanity.

These are cases with some form of positive outcome. Only too many enquiries, especially in the early days, led to the inevitable replies: 'Your father, your mother, your brother, and your sister died at Auschwitz, Buchenwald, and Dachau', or 'they cannot be traced at all.' They had been lost, as Himmler had intended they should be, in the night and fog of SS extermination.

Judgment against the SS: 1945 to the 1970s

What justice could, or still should be brought to bear on the SS and Gestapo torturers and exterminators?

This has proved to be an arduous and complex legal process. No crime of this magnitude had before 1945 ever been faced in terms of formal justice. Genocide in the past had either gone unpunished, or had been avenged through the bloodshed of war or revolution.

The Allies had declared that war crimes, and especially those of the SS, should be investigated and punished. A spectacular first trial for war crimes – the International Military Tribunal held in Nuremberg and lasting ten months from November 1945 to September 1946, judgment being completed on 1st October – placed in the dock the leading Nazis held in captivity, among them Göring, Hess, Ribbentrop, and Frank. Kaltenbrunner alone represented the hierarchy of the SS, but the real killers, Ohlendorf and Hoess, appeared at this stage only as witnesses. The trial, however, was set up as an unpre-

cedented act of international justice for an unprecedented crime – and not solely to bring justice to individuals. Certain Nazi organisations were also indicted, among them the SS, the SD, and the Gestapo. The trial took place in the full blaze of publicity. The courtroom at Nuremberg, wired with cables for microphones and for strong lighting, was adapted to serve the needs of world coverage by the press, radio, and newsreel cameras. Earphones allowed for simultaneous translation of whatever was said or read out in evidence into English, German, French or Russian.

A vast archive of captured documents, including films, was sifted and translated into the appropriate languages during the summer months of 1945 in order to supply the prosecutors with testimony for the great trial; countless interrogations were put on record, while the defence lawyers compiled thousands of affidavits on behalf of both the individual defendants and the indicted organisations. Kaltenbrunner was seen as represen-

tative of everything the SS had stood for, though behind him it was recognised that the whole system constructed round Hitler provided the framework for the crimes committed by the SS in his name. Frank, weeping with the hysterial contrition of a broken man, had to take his share of the huge burden of crime, on account of his administration in Poland.

The two most active of the principal prosecutors at Nuremberg, Mr Justice Jackson of the United States and Sir Hartley Shawcross (later Lord Shawcross) of Great Britain, did not hold back when, after the months of examination and cross-examination they and their teams of assistants had conducted, they reached their final speeches which altogether lasted four days. Mr Justice Jackson made the men in the dock responsible for all that had happened: 'No half century ever witnessed slaughter on such a scale, such cruelties and inhumanities, such wholesale deportations of people into slavery, such annihilations of minorities. The terror of Torquemada pales before the Nazi Inquisition. . . . These men in this dock, on the face of this record, were not strangers to this programme of crime, nor was their connection with it remote or obscure. . . . They are the very highest surviving authorities in their respective fields and in the Nazi state. . . . It is against such a background that these defendants now ask this Tribunal to say that they are not guilty of planning, executing, or conspiring to commit this long list of crimes and wrongs. . . . If you were to say of these men that they are not guilty, it would be as true to say that there has been no war, there are no slain, there has been no crime.'

Sir Hartley Shawcross quoted Goethe: 'Years ago Goethe said of the German people that some day fate "would strike them because they betrayed themselves and did not want to be what they are. It is sad that they do not know the charm of truth, detestable that mist, smoke and the berserk immoderation are so dear to them, pathetic that they ingenuously submit to any mad scoundrel who appeals to their lowest instincts, who confirms them in their vices and teaches them to conceive nationalism as isolation and brutality." With what a voice of prophecy he spoke – for these are the mad scoundrels who did those very things.'

When it came to the final judgment, the presiding Judges took it in turn to recite their findings. It fell to Colonel Volchkov, one of the two judges representing the Soviet Union, to read the judgment on the Gestapo and the SD, as components within the SS. He concluded with these words:

'The Gestapo and SD were used for purposes which were criminal under the Charter, involving the persecution and extermination of the Jews, brutalities and killings in concentration camps, excesses in the administration of occupied territories, the administration of the slave labour programme and the mistreatment and murder of prisoners of war. The defendant Kaltenbrunner, who was a member of this organization, was among those who used it for these purposes.'

He then enumerated all those sections of the Gestapo and SD, the members of which could be held guilty of war crimes.

The President himself, Sir Geoffrey Lawrence (later Lord Oaksey) read the judgement on the SS: 'It is impossible to single out any one branch of the SS which was not involved in these criminal activities. The Allgemeine SS [general body of the SS] was an active participant in the persecution of the Jews and was used as a source of concentration camp guards. Units of the Waffen-SS were directly involved in the killing of prisoners of war and the atrocities in occupied countries. It supplied personnel for the Einsatzgruppen [Action Groups], and had command over the concentration camp guards after its absorption of the Toten-Kopf [Death's Head] SS, which originally controlled the system. Various SS police units were also widely used in the atrocities in occupied countries and the extermination of the Jews there. The SS central organization supervised the activities of these various formations and was responsible for such special projects as the human experiments and 'final solution' of the Jewish question.

The Tribunal finds that knowledge of these criminal activities was sufficiently general to justify declaring that the SS was a criminal organization . . . It does appear that an attempt was made to keep secret some phases of its activities, but its criminal activities must have been widely known. It must be recognised, moreoover, that the criminal activities of the SS followed quite logically from the principles on which it was organized. Every effort had been made to make the SS a highly disciplined organization composed of the elite of National Socialism.

Kaltenbrunner, unlike Frank, had remained stone-faced and noncommital throughout the hearing, denying all direct knowledge of what had gone on in the camps. His argument was threadbare, but he stuck to it. He was condemned to death and executed during the night of 16th October 1946.

The other immediate post-war trials followed under the jurisdiction of the occupying powers. They were conducted against the background of the huge, hit-and-miss process of investigation known as de-Nazification which, by 1947, became increasingly a German responsibility under Allied supervision. The British alone passed some two million Germans through the successive forms of tribunal, and arrested or restricted the activities of some half million. In order to handle the principal offenders, the war criminals of lesser status than the leaders, each of the Allied powers conducted trials in their own zones. The Americans, for instance, conducted twelve main hearings, including the Action Group trial at which Ohlendorf was the principal defendant, the Doctors' trial, and the trial of the concentration camp administrative staff, at which Pohl was the principal defendant. In the British zone, one of the principal trials was that of the Belsen staff, including Kramer. Among those condemned to death were Ohlendorf, Kramer, and Bruno Tesch, whose firm had supplied Hoess with the Zyclon B gas crystals.

As the first impetus of indignation against the offenders faded, the sentences tended to grow lighter, while those condemned to long terms of imprisonment had their sentences commuted. The Germans themselves abolished the death penalty in 1949 and, like the Allies, soon grew tired of setting up trials, except in the case of men and women guilty of outright sadism and murder. The past was something only too readily forgotten in the daily need to work hard and rebuild the economy. Many once held to be war criminals were soon at large again, some of them now back in business as prosperous civilians.

The German Federal Republic, however, was to develop its own later series of trials after 1958. This was partly to solve the conscience of Germans of goodwill who wanted to prove to the world that, though Nazism was a thing of the past, known criminals who had taken part in the exterminations should not be allowed to go unpunished. Jewish world opinion, and particular that of Israel, was anxious that the murderers of the 1940s should not be free to become the respected citizens of the 1950s. Another factor was the political sniping from across the border in East Germany, where, in order to embarrass the Bonn Government, evidence would suddenly be produced against prominent officials and others in the West. The trials in Eastern Europe had been both savage and summary, but by no means comprehensive. Tens of thousands were executed or otherwise sentenced in Russia, Poland, Czechoslovakia, and East Germany, compared with 5,000 or so sentenced by Allied courts in the west and some 6,000 by the courts of the Federal Republic.

As a further gesture to Israel and the Jewish people, Germany – growing prosperous once more after years of unremitting hard work – agreed in 1952 to pay Israel DM 3,000 million to assist the country to absorb new Israeli citizens, while at the same time paying compensation to Jews who had a genuine claim against Germany for restitution, especially those expelled or driven from Germany during the 1930s and the survivors from the concentration camps.

Sporadic outbreaks of anti-Semitism and the emergence of certain extreme right-wing parties in Germany around 1960 further sharpened the German conscience to mount new, large-scale trials of the surviving, accessible war criminals. 1960, too, was the year in which Eichmann was captured so spectacularly in Argentina by Israeli agents. In June 1969 the Statute of Limitations, which controls the time limit up to which prosecutions for Nazi racial killings may be instituted, was extended from 1969 to 1979.

In 1958 a clearing-house for assembling evidence for initiating future trials at which mass-murderers would be prosecuted, was established at Ludwigsburg, near Stuttgart. From the late 1950s, the Western Allies had gradually been placing their vast archive of captured evidence at the disposal of the Bonn Government and the legal staff put in charge of the investigations leading up to this subsequent series of purely German trials set to work on the complex task of assembling the evidence and tracing the criminals still at large in Germany, or available through extradition from abroad. Many of the worst criminals were by now safely established in Latin America or in Nasser's Egypt. One of the worst of the SS doctors, Dr Horst Schumann, was found to be working for Nkrumah in Ghana, but he was not extradited until after Nkrumah had fallen from power.

The most spectacular of the many trials set up in West Germany during the 1960s was the Auschwitz trial started in Frankfurt in 1965 and lasting nearly two years. The defendants were officers and guards from Auschwitz, including Hans Stark, the schoolboy killer, Wilhelm Boger, who beat prisoners sadistically while they were suspended on a swing (the 'Bogerswing') by the crooks of their knees, Joseph Klehr, who killed hundreds of prisoners by injecting phenol into their hearts, and others, such as Emil Bednarek and Oswald Kaduk, who would club, beat or whip their helpless victims to death. Other defendants, representing the more intellectual wing of the SS were SS doctors Victor Capesius and Franz Bernard Lucas. Lucas was the only defendant who agreed to accompany the court to Auschwitz, which is preserved now by the Polish government as a permanent memorial to those who died.

The prolongation of such trials as that at Nuremburg in 1945-46 and at Frankfurt almost twenty years later may exhaust the patience of everyone involved, but the exact display of evidence and the confrontation which takes place between the public and the criminals involved are a matter of the highest social importance. Compared with this assertion of the unbelievable facts of human nature, the ultimate sentences passed on the guilty men are of little consequence. None, in any case, can be executed, and many are too old or too sick to be long confined in prison. Similarly, the trial of Eichmann in 1961 forced the world to study this insignificant man who had made such significant history. The records of his many interrogations and of the trial itself are what matter, not the sentences passed upon him or his execution. The younger generation, both German and Jewish, attend these trials and learn the truth about the potentialities of ordinary human nature. They learn too the meaning of the word genocide, a word not even included in the two-volume Oxford dictionary of 1933, the year Hitler came to power.

What, asks the younger generation of its elders, did you know of all this – and, if you knew anything at all, why did you let it happen?

Goebbels in his private diaries records his knowledge of the genocide his regime was practising. While on 7th March he still appears to think in terms of evacuating the Jews to the east, and even mentions the old pipe-dream of Madagascar as a Jewish settlement after the war, by the end of the month he has learned the truth from Hitler: 'The Jews under the Government-General are now being evacuated eastward. The procedure is pretty barbaric and is not to be described here definitely. Not much will remain of the Jews. About sixty per cent of them will have to be liquidated; only about forty per cent can be used for forced labour. . . . It's a life and death struggle between the Aryan race and the Jewish bacillus. No other government and no other

regime would have the strength for such a global solution as this.'

Although at Nuremberg Göring denied all knowledge of the genocide policy, we have seen that it was he who issued the notorious 'final solution' order to Heydrich, who had no doubt at all what this meant. Himmler's speeches to closed groups were, as we have also seen, equally revealing. The work of the Action Groups was clear enough for all those who may have witnessed them in action, and there is enough evidence that both senior officers and men in the German army knew what the Action Groups were for, if only because in many instances they complained of it. But once the work of genocide was confined to the concentration camps in the east, real knowledge of what was going on could be confined to a comparatively restricted number of people – but this number was still not negligible, and ranged from all those who had anything to do with the camps or lived near them to those who were in any way involved in the deportation of the Jewish prisoners in circumstances of such incredible harshness. Altogether, tens of thousands at the very least knew enough of what was happening by some form of direct experience, while many more knew of it by hearsay and rumour. The problem was that no one without this direct experience of the killings really believed it. No one thought a human holocaust on such a scale was possible. Jews were being transported to labour camps, and some were no doubt dying through harsh treatment. So much was universally known. But mass-genocide? The nature of the crime was not understood, neither in human nor in technological terms.

In this way it is was not difficult for 'friend' and 'enemy' alike to reject the facts as rumour. In time of war, people concentrate largely on their own work, their deprivations, and their sufferings – which were obvious enough in bombed-out Germany. When the harder evidence of genocide began to percolate through, it was equally rejected on the Allied side as quite unbelievable. If the Hungarian Jews themselves refused to believe these 'rumours' when they were being assembled for transportation to Auschwitz in 1944, why should people in Hamburg or Berlin, London or New York believe them? The German public in any case would not want to possess such incriminating knowledge, while the diaries and records of the German resistance to Hitler reveal no suspicion at all of these things. In any case, the majority of the German public in the middle years of the war seem to have been quite indifferent to the fate of the Jews.

However, an opinion poll taken in Germany during 1961 from people in the appropriate age-groups revealed that thirty-two per cent said they knew about the exterminations as against fifty-eight per cent who firmly stood by the fact that they knew nothing until after the war.

Yet the hard evidence about genocide was being brought out from the camps. Some of the instances are well enough known – Kurt Gerstein, for example, the SS officer and acquaintance of Pastor Niemöller, who continually from 1942 revealed to members of both the Protestant and Catholic churches what he knew as a supply officer in charge of the Zyclon B gas crystals. But his principal written report on the exterminations lay filed by the Swedish government, virtually unseen until after the war. In 1942 Dr Gerhardt Riegner, head of the Geneva office of the World Jewish Congress, was given hard details of the exterminations by a German businessman, and passed the information to the American and British consulates in Geneva. But the State Department withheld the information from Rabbi Stephen Wise, President of the World Jewish Congress, who only learned of it through Sidney Silverman, Chairman of the Jewish Congress in Great Britain. Months passed before the reports were officially 'authenticated'.

In Britain, Anthony Eden publicly condemned 'this bestial policy of cold-blooded extermination' in the House of Commons at the period when, in December 1942, the Allies made a joint declaration condemning extermination. If this were not in itself enough, Thomas Mann, among others, broadcast from New York on a number of occasions during the war, giving sufficient details for the public to grasp something of the truth. The broadcasts were relayed in Great Britain, and he broadcast similar talks to the Germans themselves. Then, late in 1944, the further, very full evidence provided by Vrba and Wetzler reached, as we have seen, Roosevelt, Churchill, and the Pope.

In their own way, therefore, the SS can be considered as potentially very successful in their policy. Had the war gone more favourably for Germany, it is deeply disturbing to contemplate what the gathering momentum of extermination would have produced as thousands disappeared daily in the routine of destruction at Auschwitz and at other, similar centres built on the same pattern.

The decline of the SS was in direct proportion to the decline in Germany itself. They inherited the men of the poorest quality whom Hitler could spare from his failing battlefronts, and they incorporated the waste products in manpower of the occupied countries in the form of collaborators prepared to join forces with them for what they could get out of the camps in graft and petty theft. The victims were always the prisoners, whom German society seemed ready to yield up to Himmler with scarcely a protest, while at the same time staunchly denying that they knew anything about the exterminations being undertaken in their name.

Everything which happened took place inside a dozen years, no more. In that brief space, the ruthless efficiency of the SS, and its component forces, the Gestapo and the SD, spread across the greater part of Europe. The complete plan for a similar subjugation of Great Britain came to light after the war. At the head of the administration ready to move into Great Britain was SS-Colonel Professor Dr Franz Six, formerly dean of a new faculty of political science, the Faculty for Foreign Countries in the University of Berlin. Six was another of Himmler's intellectuals, and one of Heydrich's most trusted officers.

The plan for Great Britain was prepared during the summer of 1940 under the title, *Orders Concerning the Organization and Function of Military*

The Court at Nuremberg

Government in England. Able-bodied men between seventeen and forty-five would have been despatched to Germany in large numbers for slave-labour; raw materials, plant, and equipment would have been plundered and removed. Behind the invading forces, Professor Six and his police forces would have moved in. As in Poland, the intelligentsia would have been 'liquidated' along with the Jews – the names officially listed included H G Wells, Noel Coward, Bertrand Russell, J B Priestley and C P Snow.

The list of names of victims, printed and full of inaccuracies, survives. SS and Gestapo headquarters were to be established in London, Bristol, Birmingham, Liverpool, Manchester, and Edinburgh.

It was a proud moment to find your name in the list of 'dangerous' men and women after the war, but it would have been a bitter business had Operation Sea Lion, Hitler's invasion plan for Great Britain, not been abandoned by 1941 for Operation Barbarossa, the invasion of Russia. The Battle of Britain in the air proved too expensive, and Hitler had never

liked the idea of battles at sea. The invasion of Great Britain was indefinitely postponed.

It is interesting to ponder who would have come forward to join the British contingents of the SS to help guard the local concentration camps and help with exterminations in some remote part of the island. For the most alarming fact about the SS is that it was manned, rank and file, by very ordinary men and women of many nationalities, most of them below normal intelligence, leavened here and there by sadists who reached instinctively for victims, by criminals who welcomed a quick release from jail and the chance for graft, and, above them at the 'top', by intellectuals who savoured the opportunity for power.

The SS attracted the kind of people who were in one way or another misfits in normal society, from whatever level or class or nation they might originate. They were, whatever their psychological motive, the enemies of the people, and the destroyers of their liberties. This is the final outcome of a police state, that the best must be destroyed at the hands of the worst.

Bibliography

The publishers are grateful to Alexander Bernfes for the use of photographs from his private collection

Auschwitz M Nyiszli (Panther Books, London. Frederick Fell Inc, New York)
The Burden of Guilt: A Short History of Germany 1914-45 Hannah Vogt (Oxford University Press, Oxford and New York)
Commandant of Auschwitz Rudolf Hoess (Weidenfeld and Nicolson, London. World, New York)
Destruction of European Jews R Hilberg (W H Allen, London)
Eichmann in Jerusalem Hannah Arendt (Faber, London. Viking Press, New York)
Gestapo Edward Crankshaw (Putnam, London)
Harvest of Hate L Poliakov (Elek, London)
Heinrich Himmler Roger Manvell and Heinrich Fraenkel (Heinemann, London. Putnam, New York)
Heydrich Charles Wighton (Odhams, London. Chilton, Philadelphia)
Human Behaviour in the Concentration Camp Elie Cohen (Norton, New York)
The Incomparable Crime Roger Manvell and Heinrich Fraenkel (Heinemann, London. Putnam, New York)
The Scourge of the Swastika Lord Russell of Liverpool (Cassell, London. The Philosophical Library, New York)
The SS: Alibi of a Nation Gerald Reitlinger (Heinemann, London. Viking, New York)
The Theory and Practice of Hell Eugen Kogon (Secker and Warburg, London. Farrar, Straus and Giroux, New York)
The Trial of Adolf Eichmann Lord Russell of Liverpool (Heinemann, London. Knopf, New York)